Great Girls

Profiles of Awesome Canadian Athletes

LAURA ROBINSON
and
MAIJA ROBINSON

HarperTrophyCanada™
An imprint of HarperCollins*PublishersLtd*

To all the Great Girls and Great Boys I run, cycle, and ski with at Cape Croker First Nation Elementary School.

—LR

I would like to dedicate this book to my gals and pals.

—MR

Great Girls

Published by Harper*Trophy*Canada™, an imprint of HarperCollins Publishers Ltd

First Edition

HarperCollins books may be purchased for educational, business, or sales promotional use through our Special Markets Department.

HarperCollins Publishers Ltd
2 Bloor Street East, 20th Floor
Toronto, Ontario, Canada
M4W 1A8

www.harpercollins.ca

National Library of Canada Cataloguing in Publication

Robinson, Laura
Great girls : profiles of awesome Canadian athletes / Laura Robinson, Maija Robinson. — 1st ed.

ISBN-13: 978-0-00-638559-2
ISBN-10: 0-00-638559-1

1. Women athletes—Canada—Biography—Juvenile literature. I. Robinson, Maija II. Title.

GV697.A1R62 2004 J796'.082'092271
C2004-901026-3

RRD 9 8 7 6 5 4 3

Printed and bound in the United States
Set in New Century Schoolbook

Table of Contents

Foreword

It was on a frigid Winnipeg winter day that I first stepped clumsily onto the ice that covered the parking lot of the community park. My mom held me up and, with great patience, helped me shuffle around what must have been a metre-square area of the rink. I was two and a half years old at the time, and little did either of us know this was the beginning of an adventure that would lead me around the world, on skates and by bicycle, donning the maple leaf of Canada in the world of sport.

My sister and I took to the ice as if born to glide, laughing and playing on the slick surface, falling as kids do, oblivious to the pain and loving the time with our mom. Eventually my dad flooded a rink in the backyard that felt, at the time, as big as Lake Manitoba. Looking back I realize it was barely half the size of the single-car garage behind it. We didn't care; all we wanted to do was skate.

From there I played every sport on the community club and school list available. It wasn't until another Winnipeg winter afternoon that my life would change forever. While channel-surfing I came across coverage of the Olympics on CBC sports. I witnessed speed-skating for the first time. The athletes looked larger than life with their massive legs seemingly ready to burst out of the skin-tight Lycra suits. The crouched position was deceivingly awkward until the starting pistol fired and the skaters exploded with finesse from the line. Never had I seen such a powerful yet elegant way to move.

The obvious favourite was Canadian Gaëtan Boucher, in his last Olympics, and I was to learn much about the esteemed champion in the profile shown. I was not so much impressed with his laurels as I was with his display of inner fight and determination during the race. I was fascinated and knew, somewhere deep in my core, that this was what I wanted to do. My Olympic dream began and changed my life forever.

I began to skate and with some success was recruited into cycling, knowing I would return to the ice to fulfill my dream of representing Canada at the Winter Olympics. My experiences during my ten years as a racing cyclist allowed me to return to skating with the mental and physical capacity to do anything I set my mind to.

Sport has offered me countless lessons through failure and success. It has taught me the importance of awareness, inward and outward, and the value of following my heart, my bliss, in life. My passion is skating and I have a true love for riding my bike, yet none of this would be possible to enjoy without a balance of perspective. I don't rely on results for fulfillment and haven't allowed my identity to be solely based on sport.

The following stories showcase women of all ages following their bliss, paving the way for the next generation. They are on the hero path and are breaking new ground for all of us. That most of them go unnoticed is a great loss. I've seen, and been inspired by, Hayley Wickenheiser, long after the rest of the team has left, practising rink-side for hours; I saw Beckie Scott being awarded the Olympic silver medal from the original bronze, and soon to be gold; I know, thanks to Laura Robinson, and have visited Sekwan, Takwakin, and Keewetin Trottier at their home and have been captivated by the athletic freedom and beauty of these young athletes.

As I look back and remember who I was that Winnipeg afternoon when I saw Gaëtan skate, and reflect on where I have ended up, I cannot help but feel hope when I think of the possibilities such stories offer. You never know where a glimpse into the lives of so many Great Girls may lead to.

Clara Hughes

Introduction

Welcome to the Land of Great Girls. This is a place where girls care about being good athletes, but don't ignore the rest of their life. Sometimes we get the message that you have to be perfect at everything, and we know that's impossible, so in the Land of Great Girls, we get to do all the things we love. Which includes playing sports, as well as many other things!

My name is Laura Robinson and today I am a sports writer. But I still love to ride a bike forever on a glorious summer day, ski into the deep dark woods in the quietness of a winter snowfall, or throw on a pair of runners and go for a quick run in my Toronto neighbourhood, even if I have a million other things I'm supposed to be doing. Since at least the time I was your age, I loved to be active. The only time my sister, brothers, and I weren't out skating, tobogganing, or building snow forts in the winter was when the Olympics were on television. I remember when I was nearly ten years old and watched the Winter Olympics one evening. My mom had made us hot chocolate, and we settled onto the cushions on the basement floor. It was 1968, which meant the Games were held in Grenoble, France, and that night the ski races were on. Nancy Greene was about to make Canadian history. She stood still at the top of the French Alps, trying not to think about the disappointing tenth place she had skied to in her favourite event: the downhill. All those years skiing in Rossland, B.C., had added up to these Games. Nancy gathered up all her concentration and skill and in a flash she was down the mountain. The scoreboard lit up with a very quick time. She had won the silver medal. Nancy said later that she knew, after this race, that she could win the giant slalom. In a few days we were back with our hot chocolate and Canada's great skier once again stood atop the Alps. Off she went with one confident *whoosh* out of the start gate. At the end of this race, she was an incredible 2.64 seconds ahead of second place. Nancy Greene had won the gold in the giant slalom event! There was a smile on her face when she accepted her medals. I think it said, "Try this. It's fun."

I watched the Summer Olympics a few months later and saw Elaine Tanner, who was called Mighty Mouse by the press because she was a world record holder and only seventeen, churn through the waters at the Mexico City Olympics. At the same Olympics, Bev Boys soared through the air as a diver, defying gravity. I was hooked for good. I knew I would be an athlete. I just had to figure out which sport I loved the most.

When I was fourteen I did my first bike race, and found my love. I kept at it for many years, and eventually made the national team. Years later, I had a bad bike crash and decided I would switch to rowing. It seemed a bit safer. That year I teamed up with a girl named Daniele Laumann: she was port and I was starboard in the pairs rowing shell. We didn't have great style but as a crew we gelled, and in 1979 we won the Canadian Championships.

In the winter, I always cross-country skied. I didn't make the national team or become a national champion in that sport, but I think that of the three sports, cross-country skiing has stolen my heart. Nothing matches a forest of new snow and a trail meandering through it.

Though I don't compete seriously anymore, I still love sports, but I don't read or hear about female athletes as much as I'd like to. In the fall of 2003, the Canadian women's soccer team made history at the World Cup by being the first Canadian team ever to make it to the semi-finals. To get there they beat China, one of the top teams in the world. In the semi-finals they played against Sweden, who beat them 2–1.

It's interesting to compare the way Canadian media covered the Men's World Cup of soccer in 2002 and the Women's World Cup in 2003. All kinds of sports reporters were sent to Seoul, South Korea, to write about the men's games, though Canada didn't have a team that qualified. There is nothing wrong with covering an event that doesn't have Canadians in it—soccer is an international game, after all. The problem is, Canadian newspapers gave far greater coverage to the men's World Cup than they did to the women's.

Why do sports editors and sports reporters think female athletes don't deserve equal coverage? Do they still think, in the twenty-first century, that we're not real athletes? If they do, they are out of step with the attitude of many Canadians. As Canada's women's team played against Japan (3–1 Canada) early on in the tournament, 292,000 fans turned on Sportsnet's coverage. The Toronto Blue Jays game at the same time only drew 273,000. In the quarter-finals against China, 320,000 fans tuned in, though it didn't start until 10:30 p.m. in Ontario (where the bulk of Sportsnet's audience lives). Canada won 1–0 and went on to meet Sweden, again late at night. This time the viewership went up to 703,000. The year before, when our national women's soccer team took on the United States in the Under 19 (U19) World Cup final, 914,000 fans tuned in. Sportsnet compares these figures to the 2002 NHL playoff game between the Colorado Avalanche and the Los Angeles Kings when 697,000 fans watched. So if 217,000 more fans watched the U19 Women's World Cup final than watched a playoff game in the NHL, why are the newspapers still filled with stories about male professional hockey players?

Same goes for the World Cycling Championships. Canada has one of the strongest women's teams in the world and in 2003 they competed in Hamilton, Ontario—our own backyard. But the sports sections missed this story completely. If they wrote about the Championships, it was about the great Spanish men's team, and perhaps tacked at the end of the article was "Oh yes . . . Canadian women are racing too."

Canadian girls have a wonderful history of sports heroes, but we don't know very many of them. That's why my fourteen-year-old niece, Maija Robinson, and I wanted to write this book. Otherwise, who would know, for instance, that Nora Young was playing hockey as a twelve-year-old girl on the frozen shores of Lake Superior in the 1920s with magazines stuffed into her wool stockings for padding? Nora was the only girl on the team, and were those north winds ever chilly! Later, during the Second World War, she barnstormed American arenas with a hot Canadian hockey team. Barnstorming is when a sports team visits as many towns as possible and plays as many games as possible. As a WAC (Women's Army Corps) she saw European duty during the Second World War and when she returned home, worked in northern Saskatchewan with Aboriginal people. You'd think Nora would have enough on her plate, but she also went on to win the national basketball title after the war. This all-round athlete was a Canadian champion in track and field, and in cycling as well.

In *Great Girls* you'll meet Nora and plenty of others who started playing sports when they were girls. Some are still girls, and some have grown up to be sporting women. Some played in their community while others went on to win international titles. Some had many hurdles to clear, not only as girls who weren't always treated fairly in sports, but as Aboriginal people, as African Canadians, and as new Canadians. Some had to figure out how to live their dreams in a world that still doesn't treat disabled people very well. But hurdles are meant to be cleared, and though all of the girls in this book love sports, they have another story outside of the arena. Girls who are great like to be balanced. They see sports as part of their life, but not their whole life.

Okay, okay, Laura. You've been writing long enough. My name is Maija Robinson, and I'm writing this book with my Aunt Laura. The sports that I most enjoy are swimming, snowboarding, basketball, and soccer, but I also love music, playing the piano, and playing the guitar. When I'm doing those things I feel so alive and feel like I can go anywhere!

Sometimes when I'm playing the guitar, I feel like I'm on stage, playing in front of an audience. When I swim, whether it is racing in a relay race at camp or just jumping off the pier into deep water, I am always having fun. So *Great Girls* is a place where girls get to be rock stars, racers, soccer queens, and, in snowboarding lingo, shredders of the best sort! In other words, if you like mixing sports and fun with a little imagination thrown in, you're a Great Girl. Whether it is team sports or solo, you always will be a Great Girl. The one thing I love about being on a team, though, is that you get to be with all your friends, you get to celebrate together, and sometimes you even get to have a little "après-game" party! YAY!

Ever since I can remember I have been involved in sports in some way. I've always loved running around. My mom and dad tell me I started my sports career by jumping off the small step going into our living room when I was really young. As years went by, I changed up to road hockey on inline skates, which was slightly more difficult. Then I moved to the country and could no longer play the road hockey that I enjoyed so much. Fortunately there were plenty more opportunities for me to do sports.

Last year I was on the cross-country running team and the soccer team, but the only problem was that the two seasons were at the same time. My two friends, Sarah and Kirstie, also made both teams. We started training soon after school started in the fall, and then finally we were going to the big running meet—the regional meet for the area. I was dreading this meet because I was afraid I couldn't do it. But we'd been training for almost two weeks and I was excited because I thought . . . maybe I could. Maybe the whole team could be fast.

We took a bus on a really miserable day—raining, freezing cold, and yep, we had to run 3 kilometres in this. In the end, Sarah got third, Kirstie got fourth, and I placed twelfth out of eighty-four people. Our team did very well—third place with only three girls. A few hours later that day, our school soccer team had a game. Luckily the weather cleared up and the sun even paid a visit. It was actually a super game, even though we were very tired. Our team, the Cobras, won. The whole team was cheering, especially Kirstie, Sarah, and me. We had an exhausting yet awesome day. And I felt great.

I know that you probably really want to get on with the rest of the book, but before you do I have to tell you about how I found a new sport when my best friend, Deanna, and I had a great adventure in the summer. We went to B.C. to visit my aunt and uncle in Vancouver. We had a fabulous time, but the best part about this trip was when we got to go to Long Beach. Deanna and I had the opportunity and the adrenaline rush to go SURFING! It was an unbelievable amount of fun. If you have ever been snow- or skateboarding, you will love surfing, but if you are afraid of water and waves it is not for you. Let me tell you, the fun that we had out on the waves is a memory to last a lifetime. We are not pro surfers by a long shot, but that is not important. What is important is that we enjoyed ourselves! That's what a Great Girl is—someone who does the things she enjoys because she wants to, not because someone tells her she must.

Maija and I have lots of other stories about how good it feels to try new sports, and we bet you do too! *Great Girls* celebrates the dedication and the sheer joy athletes feel while doing their sport. We hope their stories will inspire you in whatever you choose to do. Oh, and don't forget the great quizzes at the back of the book!

Hayley Wickenheiser:
On a Breakaway All on Her Own

There wasn't a time when Hayley Wickenheiser didn't play hockey. In her hometown of Shaunavon, Saskatchewan (population 2,200), just about everyone grew up with a hockey stick in their hands. Hayley was no different. She was playing hockey soon after she learned how to walk.

Hayley was born in 1978, and grew up loving rural prairie life. For years she regularly made the journey with her family to Swift Current, 50 kilometres away, to cheer on the Broncos, a major junior men's team. Since she was a little girl and knew nothing of barriers, Hayley saw no reason why she couldn't be a part of this hockey world. Saskatchewan has a fine history of raising some of the best hockey players in the country. It is a very popular sport there—despite the fact that Saskatchewan is a province with towns and villages many kilometres away from one another, and that in a fierce prairie blizzard, driving to an away game might take half a day. Everyone

I.D.E.A.S. PHOTOGRAPHY

hopes the snowstorm holds off until the players get home safely.

For Hayley, this problem of travelling long, long distances to games was compounded by the fact that there were so few girls' teams. But given how driven and practical Hayley is, these factors did not seem to bother her. From the age of five she played with boys and became a star player in their league. Hayley loved hockey and she loved Saskatchewan.

When she was twelve, however, her small-town way of life and playing at the local rink came to an end. Her family moved to Calgary, so her mother,

Marilyn, could take a job as a teacher. Girls' and women's hockey was one of the fastest growing sports in her new city, but the pace of such a big city was hard to get used to. "Actually I didn't like it at first because I wanted to live in a small town," says Hayley.

For her first year in Calgary in 1991, Hayley played on a girls' team, but she longed for the quicker, more aggressive challenge of boys' hockey, and the next year she played for a AAA Bantam boys' team. Once again she was a top scorer.

By the 1994 season at only fifteen years of age, she decided to play both boys' and girls' hockey, and tried out for the senior women's national team. To her amazement, she made the team. Hayley says she "jumped six feet in the air" when told she had been named. Calgary started to look a whole lot better to the small-town girl from Saskatchewan. Hayley skated onto international ice and soon became a phenomenon. She helped Canada win the World Championships that year in Lake Placid, New York. The score of the final game against the United States was 6–3.

When she turned seventeen, she tried out for a boys' team, this time though in AAA Midget. For the first time in her life, Hayley was openly confronted by a man who would not allow a female on his team. "I was good enough to make the team, but the coach told me he just couldn't have a girl on the team. Today, at least I respect his honesty, but it was so obvious. I was discriminated against for being female."

Hayley didn't dwell on the disturbing rejection. She decided to concentrate solely on women's hockey. She joined the Olympic Oval Program for women at the University of Calgary, where she was already training with the national team. This program was set up after the 1988 Olympics (which were held in Calgary), and offered top coaching and training to girls and women. You don't have to be a university student to play at the Oval, just a girl or woman who loves the game.

At the Canadian Championships in 1996, at age eighteen, she was named Most Valuable Player (MVP) of the tournament, a title she earned again in 1998 and 2000.

Not only is Hayley an incredible hockey player, she is also an excellent softball player. In 2000, she made the Olympic team to the Summer Games in Sydney for women's softball. Before the Olympics began, the team played at the Three Nations Challenge in Brampton, Ontario. Hayley drove home the winning run in the 10th inning against New Zealand, and the Canadian team won 4–3.

Her team didn't win a medal when they competed in Sydney, but Hayley believes the experience of being a team player is just as important. "If you're going to be part of a team sport, you have to have everyone pulling for a common goal whether you're playing or not," she said. Hayley didn't play softball as much as she wanted to, but she believes that there were better players than her on the team, and it was her responsibility to make their experience the best it could be. After all, she had already won a few World Championship medals—just in a different sport. Others on her softball team would shine, while she would keep the bench warm a little more than she would have liked.

"Probably *not* playing is one of the toughest things to do in sport—to stay positive, and even at times you have to fake it, just fake that you're happy for your teammates and be supportive. There's nothing wrong with that. It's everybody trusting everyone and putting in the work and the effort and the discipline to just be a good, solid team player."

The Olympic Games weren't held until the end of September, which is the beginning of spring in Australia. Normally in September Hayley would have been skating on a hockey rink and studying at the University of Calgary. Instead, Hayley enjoyed her experience in Sydney and had plenty of fun in the Australian sun. Soon, though, she returned to Canada and was back on her club team, the Oval Extreme.

Hayley has the kind of build that hockey coaches dream of. Women's hockey is a non-checking game, but that doesn't mean it doesn't have physical contact. At 5 feet 9 inches and 170 pounds of amazing talent, she has been a force to be reckoned with since she reached that height at age fifteen.

On the women's team she was soon rewriting the record book. By the end of the 2002–03 season, Hayley had more points from goals and assists than any other woman in the history of the national team, and today she continues to rack up MVP awards like some people rack up time on their parents' telephone.

But in 2002, just before the Salt Lake City Olympics started, members of the sports media questioned the big dreams of the Canadian women's team. The Canadian team had lost eight games against the Americans as they prepared for these Olympics. In 1998, when women's ice hockey was first introduced at the Olympics, the Canadians had been the favoured team. But they didn't play up to their abilities that year and they suffered a humiliating defeat. Hayley was on the team then and she, along with most of her teammates, cried when they lost. It wasn't very sporting of them—they received the silver medal, an honour most of us would love to win—but at least they were being honest about their feelings. They had looked forward to that day for many years, and had not realized their dream. This didn't faze Hayley. Just before the final game at the 2002 Salt Lake City Olympics between the United States and Canada, she told the media that the Canadian team would win. "They can't handle it," she said of the U.S. team she was about to play. There was too much pressure on them, she added, and they would "crack."

Despite Hayley's confident prediction, things didn't look good for the Canadian team in the final game. The referee was American and called many penalties against Canada. The media commented throughout the game that the Canadians were not being treated fairly. Often they were short one player as she sat out her time in the penalty box, but the team didn't let the refereeing get to them. They remained calm and focused on the game.

Not only did the team win with a score of 3–2, with Hayley scoring one of the goals, but also she was voted MVP for the whole Olympic tournament. The big smiles the team wore after the final whistle blew told Canadians everything they needed to know. A dream had been realized—it just took longer than expected.

Hayley and her teammates came home to great celebrations. The men's hockey team had won gold as well in their final game against the Americans. We Canadians sometimes feel like we live in the shadow of our neighbours to the south. Now it was our time to glow. Hayley was in great demand and had public-speaking engagements all over the country, but as the summer wore into the early fall, she wanted to get back to her beloved ice. She had never forgotten playing with boys when she was young and believed it was time to play against men. When she won the MVP award at the Salt Lake City Olympics, everyone realized Hayley really was the best female hockey player in the world, and if she was going to continue to challenge herself, she needed to play against better and better competition. After the 1998 Olympics, and again in 1999, she had trained with the Philadelphia Flyers at their fall training camp. At her height and weight, she was only a little smaller than Wayne Gretzky had been when he played in the NHL. So in the summer of 2002, at age twenty-four, Hayley started looking for a men's team to play on.

She didn't want to play in the lower divisions in North America such as the American League or the International League. She believed much of what passed as hockey in those leagues was violent. Playing with these guys would probably give her a career-ending injury and prevent her from improving her skills as a player. But if she went to Europe, where they play more like the Canadian women—with finesse and technique on larger ice surfaces—Hayley believed she could build on her already excellent skills.

First Hayley tried the Division I men's team in Merano, Italy, but the Italian Hockey Federation would not accept the contract she signed with the team. No women allowed, they said. Canadians saw this as crazy. The team would receive an excellent player and all kinds of attention because Hayley would be the first woman who wasn't a goalie (such as Canada's Manon Rheaume) to play in a men's professional league. Hayley's next try was with the Salamat Team in Kirkkonummi, Finland. This was a Tier II men's team coached by Matti Hagman, who used to play for the Edmonton Oilers. At first he didn't believe a woman could play in his team's league—but Hayley's abilities proved him wrong, he said once Hayley had earned her place.

Hayley was smart to choose Finland. The history of women's rights in that country is amazing. Women started voting in Finland in 1906, years before any other country, with the exception of New Zealand. Many of their sports heroes are female cross-country skiers and handball players. Hayley, who lived just 30 kilometres outside Helsinki, the capital, was adopted by the country and became a role model, not just for Canadian girls, but for Finnish girls and women as well. "Little old ladies see me in the supermarket," Hayley says, "give me a nudge in the ribs, and say, 'Hit those men, OK?' Isn't that wild? They're having fun with it, which is great to see."

But outside Finland and Canada, not everyone wanted Hayley to play. The International Ice Hockey Federation (IIHF), the governing body that regulates ice hockey in the world, wasn't too happy about a woman playing on a men's team. They haven't done anything yet to block Hayley from playing on men's professional teams, but if they did, Hayley says she'd stand up to them.

"I just don't understand that line of thinking, to be honest. My playing here doesn't somehow make men's hockey less masculine. It doesn't compromise the game or diminish it in any way. It just proves that I as an individual can play at this level. I'd like to come back. I don't see any reason right now why I wouldn't want to. Could they actually do something to block me? I don't see how. But if they tried, I'd fight it."

Hayley played centre on Salamat's third line. By mid-February 2003 she had played three games, and had scored one goal and two assists. What is really amazing is she won 82 percent of her faceoffs and averaged 13 minutes of play per game. By the end of the season she had played twenty-three games. Hayley and her coach were pleased with her playing, but she started to feel lonely. She was a long way away from her partner, Thomas Pacina, and her son, Noah. Still, there was much that was familiar. "Being in Finland is a lot like living in Canada. The snow and the cold, of course. But the people here speak English, which you don't always find in Europe, especially in smaller towns like this one.

"From a hockey standpoint, the level is pretty much what I expected. It's a pretty wide-open game, the way the women's game is played internationally. So there wasn't an adjustment there.

"Taking everything into consideration," said Hayley at the time, "I'd have to say that Finland is the best fit that I could've made."

When Hayley's season was over at the end of March 2003, the Kirkkonummi Lightning had won the league championship, which meant they moved up to the first division. Hayley tried out for the team in the late summer and once again was successful, despite the division jump. She also continued to win nearly all of her faceoffs and contributed to the team's goals and assists. But life wasn't easy in Finland, and Hayley was constantly recognized as "the girl who plays with the guys." She was a big story in the Finnish media and there was a lot of pressure on her to perform. It was tiring to always be an icon—a person who symbolizes something—instead of just a person.

In November 2003, Hayley decided she couldn't be the hockey player she had hoped she would be in Finland. She wasn't getting nearly the ice-time she deserved, and felt maybe the team management saw her not as a hockey player, but more as a way to get people to buy tickets and come to the games. That's not what she wanted to be, and she was not happy. It was a tough decision, but Hayley returned to Canada soon after the season had started.

Hayley had always expected to return home to train with the national team the year before the 2006 Olympics in Turin, Italy; she just moved her plans up one year. "I love to play," said Hayley that fall. "The passion takes over. Being able to create my own magic on the ice feels so wonderful. When you help a player score a goal, you can share that moment." Hayley believes she will be able to get those feelings back, now that she is again with her Calgary team, the Oval Extreme, and also the Canadian national team. The national team hosted the World Championships in Halifax in April 2004; in the final, Canada and the United States played to a 2–0 victory for the Canadians, and Hayley scored the first goal.

Hayley tries to be the best mother she can be to her son, and she hasn't forgotten the role her own mother plays in her life. "I could not have done it myself," Hayley said when she returned to Canada after her first season. "I owe so much to my mother and the other founders of the sport."

Hayley's mother, Marilyn, hasn't just helped to make hockey better for her daughter, she's worked for equality for all girls in Alberta. As soon as the family moved to their new province, Marilyn started as a volunteer in the Girls Hockey Calgary organization, and then in the Senior Women's League. She helped coordinate the Alberta Winter Games in 1998 and 2000, though by this time Hayley was playing at the

Olympics and had competed at four World Championships. Marilyn was working for the next generation of Hayley Wickenheisers. She also helped with educational programs for hockey and at the Stettler Hockey School, outside Calgary. Marilyn and Hayley are a mother–daughter team.

Today, hockey for girls and women in Alberta continues to grow and grow. In the 2000–01 season, 3,310 girls registered to play hockey, but the next year 4,116 girls took to the ice, and the 2002–03 season grew by another 300 girls. Hayley knows that she has inspired many of them to dream big dreams of their own. “I think we have a responsibility to develop female athletes to showcase our skills and inspire them to play,” she says. Her advice to girls is to believe in themselves and not listen to people who tell them they can’t do certain things. “Girls can do anything,” she advises. “Find what you truly love to do and work hard at it. . . . If you do something you love, it doesn’t feel like work. Try to find a way to believe in yourself when no one else does.

“Girls give up too easily. It’s acceptable still for girls to start something and then say it’s too hard. Know that there will be people who are going to knock you down. Demand as much as possible from yourself. We can do it.”

Erin McLeod:
Flying Through the Air with the Greatest of Ease

Lately she's tamed her hairstyling down a bit and plays soccer like most other people—with her hair tied back. But Erin McLeod is known for both her daring saves and daring hair. Spiked into a mohawk, in whatever colour she happens to choose for the day, her hair can give her a fearsome look. But it's her playing she should be remembered for, and the great saves she made during the Under 19 World Cup of soccer in 2002 in Edmonton. Though the U.S. team won 1–0 in overtime, Erin won the hearts of Canadians with her courageous efforts in net.

After this stellar performance, Erin looked forward to the senior women's World Cup for months as she played for Southern Methodist University and the Vancouver Whitecaps teams in the summer. The Whitecaps are part of the Women's United Soccer League, a semi-pro league that plays mainly in the United States. But in the end, while Erin was chosen for the World Cup team, she didn't play goal. Instead, Coach Even Pellerud sat her on the bench and started teammate Taryn Swiatek in net, and she played magnificently. This was a decision Erin had to abide by. “It was the hardest tournament I’ve ever been to,” said Erin afterwards. “I stayed positive on the bench, but it was still frustrating because you want to be playing. I realized I’m doing this for me, I’m happy where I am, but I still want to get better.” She realized that if the team made it, she would have one year to train for the 2004 Summer Olympics, and she believed moving to Vancouver so she could train with the Canadian national team and Coach Pellerud would be the best way to do this. School could wait a year.

Erin was born in 1983 and lived in St. Albert, a suburb of Edmonton in Alberta. She first played soccer at the age of five as a Peanut player, and she has been passionate about it ever since. Her family moved to Calgary in 1989, when she was in the middle of grade one, and Erin and her parents went hunting for a new team. She found the Pink Panthers, the only girls’ team in her age group at the time. It is hard to believe that just over ten years later, in 2002, when Erin returned to Calgary to play an exhibition game against Brazil, there were 119 teams for girls and women!

While Erin played the game at every opportunity, and liked just about any position, she didn’t play goal until age twelve, when she competed for the Willow Ridge Tigers. "They put me in net because the regular goalie wasn't there. I ended up loving the experience, and from then on I had my position."

DALE MACMILLAN / CSA

Soon Erin was chosen for the Calgary Selects, an elite team, and she had the opportunity to play against other strong teams from across the country. She is a skilled goalie who isn't afraid to make big moves to stop the other team from scoring. Diving is one of her favourites. When Erin dives for the ball, she seems to defy gravity as she flies through the air, nearly horizontal to the ground. It's amazing to watch.

"The reason I love diving so much," Erin says, "is that there is more risk—the moves are up to you. You have to be fearless. There's a lot on the line, and a lot of pressure. You have to be willing to risk everything—get out of your safety zone—if you want to be good and more successful in your game. For me, there is that much more fun to the game when there is risk involved. Everyone says 'goalies are a bit crazy.'"

Erin comes by her great athletic talent honestly. Her mother was a volleyball player in university, while her father played basketball. She has an older sister named Megan who played volleyball for four years at Mount Allison University in New Brunswick, and a younger one named Cara who is training every day for her position as an outside mid-field player in her soccer club and hopes someday to play for University of Victoria.

When Erin was thirteen, the family moved to Jakarta, Indonesia, where her father, who is an oil engineer, was transferred. She spent grades nine and ten there at the Jakarta International School and played on the school team as well as in a club league. At the end of her first year she was named All-Star Keeper.

Although Erin had to leave her friends behind in Canada, she loved the experience of living abroad. She got to try new foods and see a different way of life. But Erin had a dream—one that she had had since she was five years old: to play on the Canadian national women's soccer team. So, in 1998, after grade ten, she asked her parents if she could return on her own to Calgary to pursue her goal. They agreed that she should be able to follow her dream. Before she left Canada, at age thirteen, she had been playing on the Division I Celtics Club Team with players as old as seventeen. She returned to her old teammates and lived with her grandmother. "I call my grandma 'Roomie,'" laughs Erin. "She was really great, picking me up from practice, whatever it was I needed. Both my grandmas were like that when I was in Calgary."

Erin made the Under 19 Women's National Team when she was eighteen. This category is better known as the U19. Unlike men's soccer that has had Under 17 and Under 19 World Cups for

DALE MACMILLAN / CSA

several years, the first U19 World Cup for women was played in Edmonton in 2002. And while men's soccer has had a World Cup since 1930, senior women's soccer had its first World Cup in China in 1990. Sixty years is a long time to wait.

Many other countries have an intense and passionate relationship with soccer. In comparison, Canadians are still learning to love the game, but our women's U19 is certainly helping us with their dynamic plays. We hadn't been strong on the international scene until this team came along, but the U19 squad worked very hard preparing for the World Cup; after all, it was in their own backyard. On top of this, Canada's U19 team had passion to burn.

Before the World Cup, Erin and her team went on an international tour, tuning up for the big event. Erin earned her first career shutout against Wales at the Algarve Cup on March 3, 2002. Her second U19 shutout occurred at the France International Tournament when Canada won against Australia exactly one month later in April. By the time they returned from their international tour, the team had achieved a 9–0 record in games against Italy, Mexico, Taiwan, and Brazil.

Back home, they played a "friendly" against Brazil. (A friendly is a game two countries can play against one another, but it doesn't help them qualify for a World Cup or an Olympic competition.) Canada won the game with a 2–0 score. People across Canada and around the world were sitting up and taking notice. This new group of young women and girls was good! Brazil was one of the favourites for the World Cup along with Germany, Nigeria, and, as always, the United States.

There was growing excitement for the U19 World Cup. The media also started to buzz—could the Canadian team keep up their winning streak?

Erin was part of an awesome team at the U19 World Cup. They won all of their first six games with her in goal. When they met the United States in the final it was an exciting and tense game. Erin's family had flown in from Indonesia, even her father who had been in Brazil on business. When he heard how well the team was doing, he rushed home to watch his daughter play. The game was tied 0–0 and had to go into overtime. In the second half of overtime, Lindsay Tarpley, the captain of the American squad, scored. Erin felt crushed. She was a team player and felt as if she had let the team down. It took months before Erin realized what a great contribution she and the rest of the team had made to Canada.

"We won a silver. I used to think this was a loss," she says. "Now I realize it was a huge accomplishment. Our whole goal was to get to the final, and that's what we did. You put everything into winning the final game. But you have to realize what you've done for women athletes, and soccer in general.

"In Calgary we are promoting soccer. People recognize me and want my autograph. It doesn't seem real. We didn't expect it, not in Canada. We were *the* sports story. Before the games started we thought, 'What if it's empty?' We thought there might be a couple of thousand fans—and then the stadium was sold out. Younger girls look up to me, so I want to let everyone know how great soccer is."

Erin had become a media hit with her great hairdo. The first time she experimented with her hair was during an exhibition game with Chinese Taipei while the team was sponsored by a hair product. She kept adding more mousse to her hair until it was really spiky, so when she ran out on the field, everyone was asking what that goaltender had done to make her hair so crazy. After this, Erin became even more creative and said to herself, "Let's really do it." This time she had red dye and white dye. It took 45 minutes and two other people, but when they were finished she had a Canadian Mohawk. For the U19 World Cup, Erin sported a fearsome burgundy mohawk. The combination of her hair, her goalie gloves, and her completely fearless dives made her look impenetrable and fierce.

"I really just want to focus on playing," she says. "I don't believe in wearing makeup and that sort of thing during a game, I'm just going to sweat it off. The women on the Under 19 team aren't overly commercial. No one gets done up to play. I don't play so people will look at me. I play to win."

Though Erin is very serious about her game, she believes athletes sometimes work way too hard and lose sight of how much fun sport really is. Too often, she says, "We think, 'Go for it. Give it everything you've got. If it's not perfect, it's not good enough.' Thinking only like that can get you into trouble."

Erin looks back at her own career in soccer and says she knows personally what can happen when we take the working part too seriously. "I wanted to be light and skinny. I was obsessed with working out and hardly ate anything," she says, reflecting honestly. "I had an eating disorder. My mom sat me down and said, 'You can't do this anymore.' I didn't realize what I was doing. I kinda sat down and said to myself, 'What am I doing this for?' "

Today, Erin has left the eating disorder behind, but says all girls are under pressure to conform in certain ways. "I'm better and stronger after confronting it. But I also think it's hard to get away from that magazine image of women that we keep getting. It's tough. You have to be happy and comfortable with yourself. What you look like shouldn't matter. If you are 300 pounds and comfortable and pleased with who you are, then this matters more than being thin and still not being happy."

Today Erin is 5 feet 8 inches, weighs 154 pounds, and flies through the air with the greatest of ease. She wasn't on the front page of the country's newspapers just because she had a cool haircut. She was there because she's an excellent goalie.

After the U19 World Cup, Erin continued to play for Southern Methodist University in the 2002–03 season. She was on a full athletic scholarship and felt she needed to play her best for the university. Then in February 2003, the Vancouver Whitecaps, of the Women's United Soccer League—a North America–wide league—recruited her for goal. She played all she could for them, and also made it onto Canada's senior women's national team. Erin, like her U19 teammates Kara Lang, Christine Sinclair, Carmelina Moscato, and Brittany Timko, would be on the team going to the 2003 World Cup.

Two other goalies, Taryn Swiatek and Karina LeBlanc, were also selected, and in the end, Taryn showed such amazing prowess in goal that Coach Pellerud used her exclusively. Sitting on the bench at her first World Cup wasn't how Erin had envisioned her debut on the senior World Cup team, but she says the experience was important for her. She played a lot of games leading up to the World Cup and even sitting on the bench was a learning experience. "It was really tough, but also a really good time. There was such a positive environment. We're all friends and support one another."

Added to the excellent team spirit were the special trips Erin's parents made to the World Cup. They once again came from Indonesia. Her father was able to attend the games in Columbus, Boston, and both of the Portland games when Canada beat China and played so well against Sweden. Her mother arrived in time for these last two games as well. Erin says it was awesome to have them with her again.

When the World Cup ended, the whole team was told to take "at least two weeks away from the ball," and Erin took this to heart. She visited her sister Megan in Toronto and took it easy, maybe going for a run now and then, but mainly taking a break after a season that proved to be too long. Competing in international sport and varsity sport in the same year is very stressful. Athletes often exhaust themselves to meet the demands of competition, but once the season is over, they collapse. "Last year after the U19 World Cup I didn't take a break," says Erin. "I went back to Southern Methodist and played for them and never recovered. Once that season was over, I was playing for the senior national team. This year I wanted to be careful about how quickly I went back."

Erin decided to take this year off school and prepare for the Athens Olympics in the summer of 2004. The team set up in Vancouver and Erin fell in love with the city and the beautiful West Coast forests and vistas she found there. She trained with and shared an apartment with Sian Bagshawe, the other goalie for the Whitecaps. They had a field only a couple of minutes away where they could kick and dive after balls to their heart's content. The goalie coach for the team, Shel Brodsgaard, gave Erin a whole bunch of balls to practise with once her break was over. In November the team got together for a camp to make sure everyone was on track again, and then the hard training for the Olympic qualifier began. Costa Rica hosted the Olympic qualifier, which is a series of tournaments that selected which countries would represent North America, Central America, and the Caribbean at the Olympics.

This geographical area is referred to as CONCACAF in international soccer and only two countries out of the entire region would qualify.

But dreams don't always become realities, and after winning every game up to their semi-final, the Canadian team would ultimately lose to Mexico in the CONCACAF qualifier 2–1. With only two countries to qualify, this meant that the United States and Mexico would go to the Athens Olympics and Canada would once again stay home. Though Erin didn't play goal in this game, the impact was huge.

"I think after the game everyone was really disappointed," she says. "Going into it we all felt really pumped, really confident. But it just didn't work out for us that day. A lot of people had put their lives on hold for the next six months because we were preparing for the Olympics. All of a sudden people were saying, 'Now what?'

"Our coach Even Pellerud told us we have to see things in the long term. We have to look ahead three years from now to the World Cup and four years from now to the next Olympics. In four years, he said, we'll just be that much stronger. For now, I am happy to play with the Whitecaps, and they are happy that all the national-team athletes on the team can play for them for the entire season. We'll stay really competitive."

Nora Young:
All-Round Great Athlete

When Nora Young feels the first warm winds of spring, she wheels out her state-of-the-art racing bike and off she goes for a ride. "I've got a new bike and I haven't ridden it yet, so I'm anxious for spring," she said during one of winter's coldest days. True to form, Nora hopped on her bike as soon as she could and, just months before her eighty-sixth birthday, rode 45 kilometres in the Ride for Heart to raise funds for the Canadian Heart and Stroke Foundation.

This woman, who has been a national champion in three sports, doesn't think age should slow anyone down. When Nora was a girl in the 1930s, she borrowed bicycles before she had one of her own, just so she could feel those warm spring winds on her face. Until recently, bicycle manufacturers didn't make racing bicycles in sizes for girls and women, so as a teenager over seventy years ago, Nora rode bicycles owned by professional male bike racers at the Canadian National Exhibition (CNE) grounds.

Toronto had wooden velodromes at both the CNE and Maple Leaf Gardens that could be erected or taken down in a couple of days. A velodrome is a cycling track with banked curves that cyclists can fly around. Special bicycles are needed for racing on a velodrome. They have no brakes. In fact, if you slow down too much on the banking, you slide to the ground and end up with nasty burns and bruises. The sport is exciting, fast, and risky—three reasons Nora loved it. She raced in the women's quarter-mile event and won the Canadian Championship for that distance in 1937.

When Nora first started biking at the CNE, she would get help from the professional cyclists, climb up on one of their bikes, even if it was too big, enter a race, and usually win. Thousands of fans came out to watch the competition on the velodrome. Racing was fairly dangerous and the only protective gear the cyclists wore were leather helmets.

Once the race ended, Nora would hop on her own coaster bicycle (with one speed) and ride as fast as she could to Sunnyside Stadium, which was about 4 kilometres away, so she could play left field for one of the hot teams in the Sunnyside Ladies Softball League.

But the Nora Young sports story started even

COURTESY NORA YOUNG

Nora is in the middle, flanked by two competitors.

before she was racing around a velodrome in Toronto. Nora was born in 1917 in Fort William in Northern Ontario. She started playing hockey on her neighbourhood outdoor rink as soon as she could skate. There weren't too many other girls out there playing—this was in the 1920s—but that didn't faze her. She just shoved a couple of Eaton's catalogues under her wool hockey socks to make an instant pair of shin pads, and off she went.

"There was a rink down the street, so that's where I played," states Nora matter-of-factly. "We played until our feet were so cold, they must have been frozen. Then we'd go inside, get warmed up, and head out again. It didn't bother me if I was the only girl." Soon she moved beyond the neighbourhood rink and joined the Fort William Bronx team, an all-girls hockey team that liked to play against the Port Arthur Maroons. Later, Fort William and Port Arthur joined to form Thunder Bay, which is still a big hockey town.

When Nora was a young girl, her family moved to Toronto. Because she was growing up in the 1920s, when Canada was a young and not very prosperous country, and in the Depression of the 1930s, her father got work anywhere he could. The family moved a couple of times between Fort William and Toronto, which may have been a little upsetting for a young girl. In those days, people moved their families to wherever they could find work. This was way before people hopped on planes. Most people couldn't afford cars, which went much slower than ours do today. Added to this is the fact that in the northern part of Canada, roads barely existed. Nora's father was lucky to have a car, and he and her brother, who was old enough to work, drove to Toronto, while the rest of the family followed on the train. But Nora had her beloved sports teams in both cities, and eventually the family settled for good in Toronto.

In the 1920s and '30s the city was a hot spot for girls' sport. Nora could do as many sports as she wanted, but still she could never get enough softball. As people moved from the country to cities, groups like the Toronto YWCA tried to provide young people with opportunities to play sports. The city could be a lonely place for someone from a small town, but joining a team sport could help them break the ice. Soon Nora joined the Sunnyside Ladies Softball League and played for the junior Sierling Colts. Sierling was a tire company that liked to sponsor girls' softball, and it had both a farm team and a prestigious senior team. In short order Nora moved up to the senior team, the Toronto Supremes, and by the time she was twenty, Nora was recruited by their competitors and was playing for the top-ranked Langley Lakeside team. Perhaps your great-grandmother played against her on one of the many teams that competed at Sunnyside, such as People's Credit Jewellers, Tip Top Tailors, Orange Crush, or the Bobbie Rosenfelds (named after the famous athlete who coached them).

This was no ordinary softball league. In those days, women's teams came from all over North America to play at Sunnyside. The players were athletes who took their ball playing very seriously. It was hard to find baseball gloves for women, and because of the Depression, many players had no money. They often caught the balls with their bare hands.

The League played "under the floodlights" for the Toronto Star Trophy. Sunnyside was the first ballpark in Canada to install lights for nighttime games. People were lined up by the hundreds in the surrounding streets, trying to catch a glimpse of the game. Fans would make their way to the park on the lake with their picnic baskets in hand to make an evening of watching women's ball, and then saunter along the boardwalk under the warm night skies. It was a cheap and exciting way to enjoy an evening during the Depression. Even the movie star Mary Pickford went to these games when she was in her hometown. In 1934, Alexandrine Gibb wrote a column for the *Toronto Star* called "No Man's Land of Sport." In it she wrote, "[T]here is still no softball or baseball league in women's or men's divisions which amassed gate receipts to equal Sunnyside."

But while Sunnyside was a popular spot for ball playing, sometimes Nora's team travelled to other stadiums to take on their rivals. "In 1937 we went to Madison Square Gardens in New York and played the New York Wolverettes," recalls Nora. "We always had a good time, and the fans were great."

Nora played in the era called "Canada's Golden Age of Sports," which lasted from the 1920s to just after the Second World War. Canadian women were some of the best athletes wherever they competed in the world. It was a fantastic time to be an athlete and to be female. Companies sponsored teams and treated the women on those teams like semi-professionals. They could work for the company, but got time off to play. There were trips all over North America, and the players wore snazzy uniforms and special clothes like leather jackets and crisply pleated pants for travelling. During the Second World War, in the United States, a professional women's baseball league was formed called The All-American Girls Baseball League. Fifty-five women from Canada played in the league. Most of them came from Saskatchewan, but a number of players from Sunnyside also played pro ball for the league.

For those who stayed in their own Canadian leagues, there were still excellent facilities and coaches, and trips to play the Americans. One trip Nora particularly liked when she played in the Sunnyside League was a tournament at a big fair in Chicago in 1937. "We played in the World Softball Tournament," says Nora. "It took us two days to finish that game. . . . It started to rain the first day, so it got held over until the next. We won 1–0 in the final."

She returned to the United States during the Second World War as a basketball player. "I played for the Simpsons Volunteers," she says. "It was a specially formed all-star team that took on Canadian, American, and Mexican teams to raise money for war victims. Those teams also came up to Canada to play us. We competed at the CNE Coliseum. It was a packed house each time."

She also went back to Madison Square Gardens on a joint hockey team made up of the top players from Toronto and Montreal. Once again, they played to a packed house. Players were still using Eaton's catalogues for padding, and the play was rough. "There was checking in those days, and we didn't use helmets," she says. "We played fast and hard." These games raised plenty of funds for the war effort, but Nora wanted to do more for her country. Eventually she decided to drop sport for a while and enlist.

In 1943, Nora joined the Canadian Women's Army Corps. She was sent overseas, but even though she worked in war-torn areas, she never thought of herself as brave—just doing her job.

Right after the war, it was her job to escort the most wanted war criminal from Germany to prison. His name was Kurt Meyer and he had ordered the killing of many Canadian prisoners of war. At the time Nora didn't know how famous he was. "I never really thought that this was very significant at the time," she says, "but he really was a terrible man."

Like many Canadians, Nora stayed after the war ended, delivering food and blankets to people who no longer had homes. But she came home to her beloved sports as soon as she could. In 1948 her basketball team, the Montgomery Maids, successfully brought the Underwood Trophy back to Eastern Canada when they won the Canadian Championship. Since 1920, the legendary Edmonton Grads had won the trophy each year. Unfortunately for the Grads, their gym had been turned into a military base, and they eventually disbanded. No western team could match them, and the Maids were powerful enough to win the Cup. In 1998, the Montgomery Maids celebrated the fiftieth anniversary of their victory. All of them were still alive and came to the celebrations!

If this weren't enough, Nora also liked to enter bicycle races—the longer the better. While she liked the excitement of the velodrome at the CNE, and rushing off to her softball game afterwards, she also loved road racing. She entered a 50-mile (about 80 kilometres) time trial on her one-speed bicycle in 1937. She finished in 2 hours, 38 minutes—after stopping to remove her sweatsuit when she became too warm, and taking a break for a cup of tea. "I passed quite a few guys who couldn't make it," she laughs. "They were on the side of the road, not looking very good."

But many changes occurred in sport after the Second World War, in the 1950s, when women were expected to stay home and be content raising children. There were a lot of male athletes who did not like being defeated by a woman. In no time, many of the arenas and playing fields that had been open to women shut them out. They were told that the men had come home from the war and they needed their ice and fields back. Just like the women who became mechanics and engineers and contributed to the war effort, and then were let go once the men started to return from the war, female athletes were sent packing. Even the beloved Sunnyside Stadium was plowed under for a private club.

Nora worked as a lab technician from the 1950s to the 1970s, and then retired early at age fifty-four, because of arthritis. "People think I just bounce back," she said once, "but I've had arthritis for years. I couldn't hold the equipment in the lab properly, and so I had to retire. But this was the time when women were getting into sports again, and I said to myself, 'Why not?' Sometimes when you like what you're doing, the arthritis pain goes away. I hopped on my bike and joined the Cycling Women's Committee of the Ontario Cycling Association, and before I knew it I was racing again in my seventies! I loved it."

Nora was part of a large movement of women into sport in the 1970s, when women started to stand up, once again, for their rights. Soon she was back on her bike, riding for fun, and in 1985, she started competing in various sports for seniors all over North America. "I'd go to the championships, thinking I would go in the bike race," she says, "but I'd get there and say to myself, 'Well, how am I going to spend the rest of my time when I'm not racing?' So I'd sign up for baseball throw, javelin, discus, football throw—you name it, I threw it. I'd end up coming home with at least ten medals from each games!" Today Nora holds seniors' state records in Florida, Michigan, New York, Arizona, Texas, and Louisiana, and no one can touch her in all of Canada.

When she turned eighty-five in 2002, women cyclists from all over Ontario came to Toronto to celebrate. Nora was the life of the party, but she didn't tell any of the guests that she had pain in her legs, especially below the knees. Later she admitted, "I said to my doctor, why don't I have strength walking, but I feel great on my bike?" And people always want to know how she does it. "Sometimes people follow me around after my event is over. They want to know what my secret is. There's no secret, for Pete's sake. Eat well. Sleep well. Get off your butt and get moving. You've got to keep moving. I've got arthritis, and they don't know how much I hurt.

COURTESY NORA YOUNG

"But I'm a participant more than a spectator. I'll be watching a game, and before I know it, I'm saying, 'Why didn't you get that ball?' and I'm in the game in no time. I don't like sitting."

To girls, Nora's advice is just as direct. "Don't let anyone put you down. Keep on going. Just keep on pushing and don't ever give up. You'll have a great life."

Clara Hughes:
Making Olympic History

She is unmistakable with her long, bright, beautiful red hair and strong build. When Clara Hughes has her helmet on and stands in her cycling shoes with cleats that elevate her even higher, she's nearly six feet tall. In the winter, when she tears around on her speed-skates, she is equally formidable!

Clara Hughes, born in 1972, became the first Canadian and the fourth athlete in the history of the Olympic Games to win medals in both the Summer and Winter Olympics. She took the bronze medal in the 5,000-metre speed-skating race at the 2002 Salt Lake City Olympics; six years earlier she had won two bronze medals at the 1996 Atlanta Olympics in the 104-kilometre road race and the 30-kilometre time trial event. And it all started in chilly Winnipeg, Manitoba.

Clara was quite a sociable little girl, always outside playing with other children, but she tried the indoor activities of gymnastics and ballet as well. Her best friend was quite natural at these activities, but Clara thought of herself as a little klutzy and did a lot of laughing in those classes instead. She was always solid and tall and felt clumsy compared to her petite friend. Ballet would not be her forte.

Soon Clara switched to soccer and ringette, and believed she had found her niche. She played both sports until she was fifteen. Then she discovered speed-skating. Once she laced those skates on and learned how to push off on their long blades, there was no holding Clara back, not even training outdoors in Winnipeg's frigid winters. Clara jokes that there must be something in the Winnipeg water—so many of Canada's top speed-skaters are from there.

Clara says she was inspired by the 1988 Calgary Olympics. "I remember watching Gaëtan Boucher skating and saying to myself, 'I want to do that. I want to skate and go to the Olympics.'" Gaëtan had won two medals in the Sarajevo Games before Calgary. In the fall of 1988, after the Calgary Olympics, where Gaëtan was the hometown favourite, sixteen-year-old Clara trotted down to the Winnipeg Speed Skating Club with her hockey skates and tried the sport out. She was instantly hooked. That first year, she was sixteen years old, Clara won a silver medal in the 800-metre race at the National Junior Championships.

In the spring of 1991, the Manitoba Cycling Association asked Clara and her teammates if they wanted to try their sport during the warm months. (Speed-skaters and cyclists use many of the same muscles in their thighs, so often try out each other's sport.) If they were accepted by the coach, they could go to a training camp in South Dakota for over two weeks to prepare for the Western Canada Summer Games.

Clara went down to the United States a speed-skater and came home a cyclist. She got up first thing the morning after she arrived back and began training on her bike. She won a number of

ANONYMOUS

medals at the Western Canada Summer Games, and went on to her first Canadian Cycling Championships on the track, where she won the 3,000-metre individual pursuit and points race. In 1992, Clara went to her first national road championships, where she won the road race and the team time trial. Clara figured it was time to hang up the speed-skates—at least temporarily. She was crazy about riding her bicycle.

In two years she was on the national team, and in 1993 went to her first World Championships, where she placed sixth in the 3,000-metre individual pursuit, an incredible performance for such a young, rookie rider. But it was in 1994, at twenty-two years of age, that she really broke into the international ranks, when she was selected to race on the Canadian team at the women's Tour de France. This race is nearly three weeks long, and takes cyclists all over France. Like the men's Tour de France it goes up and down mountains and through small villages as cyclists compete in perhaps the toughest athletic event in the world. People line the sidewalks and watch from cafés and close down their stores, just to cheer the racers on each day. The times for each cyclist's daily races are added together to figure out the overall champion.

During the first day of racing Clara established herself as one of the fastest time-trialists in the world. Time trials are racing events where riders go out one at a time on a designated course, usually 1 minute apart. Normally the course is fairly flat, and cyclists use special aerodynamic bikes and helmets to help cut down on wind resistance. Clara, with her extremely strong legs and fantastic endurance, was equally formidable in long races. She would often try to sprint away from the rest of the cyclists when there were only a few kilometres left in the race. She was so fast, very often no one could keep up with her, and she'd cross the finish line on her own in victory.

There is a tradition in bicycle races spread over several days: the fastest cyclist of each day gets to wear the prestigious yellow Leader's Jersey—*le maillot jaune*. Clara took it on the very first day when she had the best time in a short but very fast time trial. She kept it for the first three days, when the race routes were long and fairly flat, and then passed it to her teammate Anne Samplonius, who led the race for the next two days. By racing so well together for the first five days, Clara and Anne put the Canadian team in first place. It was an incredible accomplishment considering they were up against the fastest women in the world.

By the end of the Tour, only the Russian team was able to surpass them, and the Canadians ended up second overall.

Even before this, Clara had represented Canada at the 1993 World Cycling Championships on the track in the 3,000-metre pursuit. This race pits two riders against one another, with one on one side of the cycling track and the other directly opposite her on the other side. Each must ride 3,000 metres. It is terribly exciting, as cyclists who are well matched in speed will be fractions of a second either ahead or behind one another. If a rider is really fast, sometimes she actually catches the other rider.

These championships were held in Hamar, in Norway—the country that was going to host the speed-skating events at the 1994 Lillehammer Olympics. After her bike race Clara went down to the oval and stood inside. It was built like a Viking ship. The sheer size took her breath away, and she reconsidered her decision to hang up her skates. The graceful sport was really her first love. She said to herself, "Some day I will return to skate here."

Clara never forgot her promise, but for the next few years she was still a full-time cyclist. In 1995, she came second in the 30-kilometre time trial at the World Championships in Colombia. Clara had become famous in Europe, but it wasn't until the Atlanta Olympics in 1996 that Canadians finally started hearing about her. She became the first Canadian to win a medal at those Olympics with her bronze in the road race.

"I've dreamed since I was twelve that I would go to the Olympics," she said after the race. "I wasn't dreaming about winning a medal, just about being here. Then to win Canada's first medal, that is very special. I never thought I would be the first to win. Now the challenge is to leave this behind and concentrate on the time trial, because I feel like a little kid at a circus."

Later Clara said she knew on the morning of the road race that she could do something special. "I felt like I had every Canadian's hopes on my shoulders, but they were giving me energy, they weren't making me nervous. It was as if thirty million people were helping me have a great race. The feeling was incredible, but I was pretty sure I could do it."

Somehow Clara managed to calm herself down and get ready for the time trial. It was two weeks later and on the same course as the road race. She felt ready for a really good ride that day too, and to make it better, her mother and father had arrived in Atlanta to cheer her on. She had another amazing race, placing third once again. When she looked at the scoreboard, Clara was over the moon. "I thought I was going hard," she said, with her non-stop smile. "But a guy with a Canadian flag ran beside me up the hill on the backstretch and I figured I better move it up one gear. He gave me just a little more confidence to dig a bit deeper."

Clara left the Olympics while she was still somewhere near the moon, but she came crashing to Earth soon after. She had felt an old injury to her Achilles tendon flaring up while she was training for the Games, but had managed to train by regularly icing her heel and ankle. However, as soon as the Olympics were over, the affected area gave out. Many athletes injure the Achilles, which is the tendon that extends behind the ankle and connects the calf to the heel. Usually it is injured by a combination of an injury that doesn't heal properly and overuse when athletes try to train before the tendon fully recovers. This was the case for Clara. Her enthusiasm for cycling had overtaken her good judgment. She should have let her body heal. Soon she couldn't ride at all. She took many months off, but when she tried to start the season in 1997, her injury became even worse. "I thought I was going to have to end my career," says Clara. "I wasn't sure I would ever be able to even ride my bike for fun."

The 1998 season was equally awful. Clara ended up with casts on both legs as she tried to heal from what seemed to be a never-ending injury. Finally, in 1999, she found a naturopath in France who treated her successfully with a combination of minerals, physiotherapy, and massage.

By the time of the 1999 Pan-American Games, which were being held in her hometown of Winnipeg, she was ready to try racing again. Even though she didn't feel quite recovered from the past two years of injury, she placed fourth in the time trial. Two months later were the World Championships, and she believed she would be back on form by then. But the championships were in Italy, and as Clara trained on a road there just six days before her race, she was hit by a car. Nursing plenty of cuts on her badly bruised body, she raced anyway, and placed an astonishing sixth. Clara Hughes was back—or so she thought.

The next year at the Olympics in Sydney, Clara caught a nasty virus that she couldn't shake off for the three weeks before the Games. Considering how lousy she felt, her sixth place in the time trial was just as incredible as her sixth place the year before. It was four years now since she'd won her double Olympic medals, and she'd endured injuries and illness for much of that time. Clara, however, always takes everything in stride, and the strides would soon be getting longer.

In the fall of 2000 Clara moved to Calgary. That's where the Canadian Olympic speed-skating oval is located. It was time to act on the promise she had made to herself in 1993. Once again she was amazing when she managed to qualify for the national team in her first year back in the sport. She'd been away from competition for ten years. Clara credits her coach, Xiuli Wang, who came to Canada from China and held World Championship titles herself when she skated. By the end of the season, Clara had become one of the top eleven speed-skaters in the world in the 3,000-metres category.

The next year she closed in rapidly. During the week between Christmas and New Year's Eve in 2001, Clara skated the fourth fastest time ever recorded by a woman in the 5,000 metres, and was getting pretty fast in the 3,000—though she prefers the longer event. Athletes in her sport had spent years and years to skate such times, and here was Clara doing them in less than two years! Two months later, in February 2002, the Winter Olympics in Salt Lake would begin, and Clara was getting faster with each international race she entered.

Her first race at Salt Lake was the 3,000 metres, which wasn't her strongest event. Still, she and many other skaters broke the Olympic record, and eventually Clara placed ninth, while her team-mate and another Winnipegger, Cindy Klassen, won the bronze. This time Cindy won the first Canadian medal of the Games. It was a wonderful way to kick off the Olympics, and things just got better, as Clara matched Cindy's bronze in the 5,000 metres. The problem was, Canadians saw only the last few laps of Clara's race.

Instead of broadcasting Clara's competition from start to finish, CBC television decided a men's hockey game between two European teams was more important. Imagine what must have happened in the CBC's broadcast booth when news arrived that Clara was skating fast enough to win a medal! The CBC had to make a switch quickly, but we only saw bits and pieces of Clara's race until the last four laps.

Clara's mom, Maureen, was at home trying to watch her daughter race on TV. She was terribly frustrated as hockey came on instead. Clara's mother knew that she usually excelled over the last half of the race when so many others start to fall apart. Finally, the cameras switched to her race. Maureen could see Clara was going to have a good finishing time—but a medal was astounding. She was so proud of her daughter.

Clara had skated the race of her life, knocking 7 seconds off her fastest time in the 5,000. She gasped when she looked at the time, and then hobbled over to her coach and fell onto a bench. As Coach Xiuli Wang undid her skates, Clara mumbled, "I want my mom." The effort it took to win the bronze had caused a lot of pain. She would recover, but right after the race, all she could think of was cuddling up with her mother.

All of Canada cheered when Clara jumped up and down on the podium that evening after she received her medal. Then in the summer at the Commonwealth Games she won a gold medal in the time trial. After this, Clara and her husband, Peter Guzman, rode their bicycles from Dawson City to Inuvik in the Arctic Circle. What a trip that was! But once fall arrived, it was time to put away the bike and bring out the blades.

MARION WALROB

Clara's 2002–03 speed-skating season was even

faster than her Olympic year. She won several medals at the World Cup and World Championship races, including a gold in the 3,000—which wasn't her best event—in Erfurt, Germany, and a gold in the 5,000 metres at the all-round World Championships. In the summer at the Pan-American Games in the Dominican Republic, Clara won bronze, silver, and gold medals in cycling, and then decided she had had enough of trying to do two sports internationally. It was one of the hardest decisions for her because she loved cycling so much, but her heart was really on the ice, and cycling would have to be a recreational sport for her now, not a competitive one. Constantly travelling around the world and expecting herself to produce top results at international competitions year round was too much for Clara to endure. With a tear or two she retired from Canada's national cycling team in August 2003.

By early September she was back on the ice at the Olympic Oval in Calgary, slowly getting the feel of the long blades once again. That year the World Cycling Championships were held in Hamilton, Ontario, on roads that Clara had practised on for years when she moved there from Winnipeg to train in a warmer climate and on hillier terrain. She had a good chance of winning a medal—even a gold medal—in the time trial, but instead she took the opportunity to write to her friends.

"Today is the day that I thought would be my last chance to compete for the coveted rainbow jersey of the world cycling champion. This afternoon the time trial event in Hamilton, Ontario, takes place," Clara wrote. "Instead, I sit in the kitchen of my winter abode in Calgary, and wait to check the time-splits via the Internet. That I made the choice not to compete, in the World Championships or the sport again, does not disappoint me. I am exactly where I want to be, living my dream, in the realm of speed-skating. What motivates me now is watching my close friends, many of whom are former teammates, line up today and give it their all."

In March 2004, Clara achieved yet another milepost. At the World Single Distance Championships, she took gold in the 5,000. Truly she was one of the world's most accomplished athletes.

The cycling, the skating, the making of such good friends all around the world thanks to her sport—all have gone beyond her original dreams as an athlete, says Clara. But, she adds, girls need to learn "not to limit themselves and not to let others limit them. The world is full of people who will tell you that you cannot do something for whatever reason. If you have the courage to dream, anything is possible.

"I have never listened to others when they doubt me. I always surround myself with people who believe in me, and have gone beyond what I ever dreamed of achieving as an athlete. It is an inspiring way to live, for yourself and others."

Sekwan and Takwakin Trottier: Paddling Their Grandfather's Path

Sekwan Trottier's first big trip in her mom's canoe was 160 kilometres long. In 1997 she was five years old, and according to her mom, she sat down on one of the portages, put her head in her hands, and cried, "How many more suffering portages do we have to do?" But today Sekwan remembers only good things from that trip that went from Deception Lake to Lac la Ronge in Saskatchewan.

Canoeing is in the bones and blood of the Hamilton-Trottier family. Sekwan's mother, Bonnie Hamilton, was born and raised on her parents' trap-line, approximately 500 kilometres north of Saskatoon, Saskatchewan. If her family needed to get around, they used canoes, or snow-shoes, or dog-sled, or they walked.

In the summer of 2002 the family paddled really far to a northern trap-line. "It took at least nine days to get back," Sekwan moans. "It was so hot out there, and I had to take care of all the bags. I was the bag person."

Even though Sekwan complains, her mom, and

her dad, Tim, believe she'll be a better person if she has a strong body, mind, and soul, and there's nothing like a journey through the wilderness to strengthen all three. Children can learn their place on the Earth, Bonnie says, when they are being a part of the natural world, not living separately from it. Learning to be physical should not involve being in a car and driving somewhere in order to do a little hike. The family lives 400 kilometres north of Saskatoon, outside the town of La Ronge. Kids who grow up in the North, like Sekwan, her sister Takwakin, and their older brother, Keewetin, live in a peaceful, quiet world where they are a part of the natural order of things.

Today, Sekwan, whose name means "Spring-time" in Cree (she was born in April), Takwakin, and Keewetin canoe all summer and dog-sled race and cross-country ski race in the winter. Tak-wakin's name means "Autumn," as her birthday is on October 10. Her brother's birthday is on the same day, and his name means "Strong Wind from the North." Shortly after this time people in La Ronge look for the first snowfall. Because win-ter can stay for many months, and the lakes and rivers take a long time to thaw, the kids are always itchy to get in the canoe each spring, even though they ski until the last bit of snow is gone.

For instance, when she was eleven, Sekwan did her first paddle on her own across Potato Lake, which is just outside her back door, even though there were plenty of waves. She also has more responsibilities during the portages now—like taking care of all the bags she complains about! While she and her mom did a big nine-day canoe trip that same year, most of their canoe trips range from one to four days in length. And now Takwakin is the one who has to learn to carry extras.

"The last time I went with my mom in the canoe, I was in the front," says Takwakin, who is seven. "But I had to carry everything! I was so tired, but I did it. I'm the third tallest in my class."

BONNIE HAMILTON

Sekwan and Takwakin Trottier

Bonnie and Tim take their family on plenty of different routes, not just to enjoy canoeing, but to live close to the land. They fish, and if the season is right, pick blueberries. They learn how to survive in the woods and live with the land. But no matter what the lesson or canoe route, the voyage the kids like best is the one that winds to their grandparents' trap-line. The children lost their grandfather, Kimosum, to cancer in 2001, and one of the ways they remember him is to paddle the rivers he loved so much. When the Hamilton-Trottier kids used to paddle to Kimosum's home, Sekwan recalls, he always had their favourite boiled caribou ribs waiting for them.

The rivers and lakes in Saskatchewan have provided the Cree people with a livelihood for as long as rivers have flowed in the North. Every time the Hamilton-Trottier family paddles them, the kids find out more about who they are and the traditions they come from. Without realizing it, they're learning that canoeing has a history that extends far beyond the time when Europeans arrived in this part of the world. They learn about how a well-built canoe can transport so much more than its weight, and how to keep it upright by using one's weight and paddle even if the water is a bit wild. The kids have learned how Aboriginal people perfected the art of canoe-making so many hundreds of years ago. They are paddling through history each day they go out.

Another great thing about canoeing, says Sekwan, is the way it can make one forget about everyday problems. A paddle slicing through water is a beautiful sound, and when a canoe balances perfectly as it glides down a river, it feels like there can be nothing wrong in the world. Bonnie says once they are out on the water, the bickering between her kids ends, and by the time they reach their destination, everyone shares a peace of mind.

Once you've set up camp, nothing beats sitting on a rock and watching the sunset with the feeling of a day's worth of paddling in your muscles and heart. In the height of summer, says Bonnie, if you get up in the morning and go back to the same rock, it will still be warm from the day before. You just sit there, watch the sunrise, and dig your bare feet in the sand.

When the rivers freeze and the kids are no longer able to paddle, they switch to their other favourite sports—cross-country skiing and dog-sledding. Their grandfather used to come and watch; now their Aunt Hope and Uncle Sam often come down to see them participate. In the cold of winter, the waters that normally rush through northern Saskatchewan freeze and provide smooth surfaces to race dog-sleds. The race can become particularly exciting because at any given time, the dogs may run too close together. Takwakin is just learning how to race now, but even at age seven, she's been at it for a couple of years. "My dad gets mad sometimes because the dogs get tangled up in a big knot. They jump and go under each other. Then I have to stop and he rushes over to untangle them. You've got to hold on to the dogs really hard. But sometimes I can't. Sometimes I can't even get them going. I yell at them and they don't move."

The family has fourteen sled-dogs, and Takwakin is responsible for Wapisk (White) and Tipiskaw (Night) for her sled. For now she races with just two. But she must also make sure that Waskwiy (Birch), a younger dog, is fed and healthy. Keewetin and Sekwan have four to five dogs each on their sleds, so it's pretty noisy in the morning during breakfast! Many of the dogs in Northern Saskatchewan understand Cree, as this is often the language spoken, not just in communities, but in the dog-sled racing circuit in which many Cree people participate.

Sekwan's dogs are named Maskwa (Bear) and Thotin (Wind). She's able to race with up to five dogs now as she gets more strength in her upper body, and she has come to be known as "a strong-voiced girl" when she yells at her dogs to get going. *"Sohki!"* says Sekwan in Cree. It means "Faster!"

The Hamilton-Trottiers live in a household where everyone has to haul water and wood. In order to be a family they have to work together. Because they don't want to be a burden on the land, their house has no running water. If they want to go to the washroom, they have to head to the outhouse, no matter how chilly the north winds are outside. The family doesn't want to rely on too many modern conveniences, but does have a busy life combining paddling, skiing, dog-sledding, and school. Sometimes one person is coming in from feeding the dogs while another is going out to dump the water from doing the dishes. The kids know what is expected of them if they want to go dog-sledding and canoeing. No fun until the work's done.

Right now, Takwakin and Sekwan love Nordic skiing even more than dog-sledding, and have become two of the fastest girls in Saskatchewan. They started skiing because both of their parents ski, and there is a club at their school, Gordon Denny Elementary. There are two kinds of Nordic skiing: classic and skating. Classic is also called "diagonal striding" and is the ancient form of skiing that has been done in Scandinavia since the Ice Age. The skier puts the left arm forward while the right leg kicks back, and then as the right leg comes down to kick the ski against the snow, the skier shifts weight and the left leg does the kicking while the right arm extends forward. It's a lot like walking, but when it's done properly, it looks as smooth as a perfect ballet. Skate-skiing is more modern and skiers literally move on their skis as if they are on skates. This technique is faster, but it needs a wider trail as skiers extend their skis farther out.

At the 2003 Provincial Championships, the Trottier girls walked away with two medals each. In the Atom age division, seven-year-old Takwakin took bronze in her 1-kilometre classic skiing event and gold in the 1-kilometre skate-ski race. Sekwan, who is in the Mini-Midget category, finished with a silver in the 2.5-kilometre classic event, and won gold in the skate race. "I practised my hills a lot this year," she said after the race, "and there was a hill called Heartbeat. It's the hardest one on the whole course. The girl who beat me in the classic was beside me when we started climbing. But when I looked back at the top of the hill, she was still at the bottom. I just went as hard as I could, and won."

In 2004, just before she turned twelve, Sekwan again dominated the Provincial Championships. She skied to a gold in the 3-kilometre skate in a time of 15:36, and a silver in the 3-kilometre classic with a finish of 17:01. "I was really scared at the start of the skate event because it was a mass start," says Sekwan. "I was really tingly, and I was scared I was going to come in second because I had a really bad cold. But I won and then we went tubing and that was so much fun."

Sekwan also earned a special reward because it was the second year in a row she had won silver and gold at the Provincial Championships. Cross Country Saskatchewan gave her $250 to use for out-of-province racing. Sekwan travelled to Alberta to race at Sharkfest, on Mount Shark, in the Rocky Mountains. This event attracts top racers from the host province and B.C. and is particularly challenging because racers compete at a high altitude and must climb significant grades, but Sekwan was up to the challenge, placing in the top six in both of her races.

Takwakin is following quickly in her older sister's ski tracks. "I love skate-skiing," says Takwakin. "Going fast makes me feel like I'm flying. Sometimes all I want to do is skate-ski because it makes me fly the best." If anyone can fly on a pair of cross-country skis, it's Takwakin. She's always chasing after her brother and sister, and can usually stay with them for the first 3 kilometres of their ski. When she was only six years old, she entered the 20-kilometre event at the La Ronge Saskaloppet, a cross-country ski tour in her hometown. At the start line the thermometer read –30°C. Many grown-ups wouldn't have ventured out in such weather, but it didn't faze Takwakin.

"It was windy on the lake," she says of the starting area for the loppet (which is a ski tour or race that everyone starts at once), "and it made me tired. But I kept going and I felt good. My mom kept saying, 'Keep on going,' and we stopped at all the checkpoints and ate food and drank water. When I'm eight I'm going to do the 35-kilometre race." In 2002, Takwakin won the prize for the youngest skier and received a beautiful pair of beaded moose-hide moccasins. While Takwakin skied 20 kilometres with her mother, Sekwan did the 35-kilometre event, gliding beside her father, Tim. Keewetin is old enough to ski the 55 kilometres on his own now. Sekwan's dad says it's only a matter of time before he won't be able to keep up with his daughter. "She was already dropping me on hills," he said, exhausted when he hit the finish line after skiing with Sekwan in the 2003 loppet.

In 2004, Takwakin had moved into the Pee-Wee

(eight to nine years) category. She mirrored her older sister's results at the provincials and also took home silver in the 2-kilometre classic event and gold in the 2-kilometre skate. But it's tough to follow in the very fast tracks of her older siblings (Keewetin won two medals too), and sometimes, says Takwakin, she's a little tired of it all. "When my legs start to hurt and stuff in the race, I get a bit bored. But I like skiing. You have fun, and I like the flats the most. It feels like I'm not even touching the ground. Inside I feel really happy."

She also skied in the 20-kilometre event at the Saskaloppet and again won her age division. In 2003 she had completed the race in 4:38. In 2004 she clocked in at 3:25. She skied the first half with her mother and the last with her father. "Last year my main concern was to get her going," says Takwakin's mother, Bonnie. "This year I just wanted to try to keep her in sight."

Sekwan, Takwakin, and Keewetin are all good friends of speed-skater and cyclist Clara Hughes and update her through e-mail on their training. They met her when they were in Calgary because they were all in the same play about sport that was put on by the University of Calgary.

Clara and the kids had fun during the play and soon Clara became "Auntie Clara" as she took them to speed-skating races and got them to try skating with her. Later she came to Sekwan's birthday party. But something special happened between these friends in 2002. On the same day that Clara won a bronze medal in speed-skating at the Olympics in Salt Lake City, Sekwan won two silver medals at the Saskatchewan Provincial Nordic Ski Championships.

Just before Clara's event, the kids in La Ronge e-mailed her and told her to think about the word *ikwa*. It means "now" in Cree, and it is what their mother tells them when they have to go hard. Their advice seems to have paid off. Clara wrote the word on her hand so she could be reminded of it during the race. Now Clara updates them on her training and they update her on theirs. "Clara trains on ice, and I train on snow," says Sekwan, "but lots is the same. I want to get speed-skates. I like Beckie Scott, Kendra Ohama, and Georgette Reid too."

Sekwan, Takwakin, and Keewetin like to look up to older athletes as role models, whether they be from a national team or a high-school team. Because of their amazing success, they have started to train with the high-school kids in the La Ronge Ski Club. It's not all work, though, says Takwakin with a big grin. "We mainly like to have snowball fights with each other."

Angela James:
A Lone Pioneer

Flemingdon Park may not be the first place people think of when they imagine the origins of a great Canadian hockey star. There wasn't even a rink in this large housing complex by the Don Valley in Toronto when Angela was growing up. But there have always been enough roads to have constant road hockey games and plenty of kids. Angela dreamed about becoming an Olympic hockey player some day.

Angela, who was born in 1964, and her four brothers and sisters grew up here with their mother, Donna. Of all the sports that were played on the roads and in the parking lots of the housing complex, it was hockey—on the street or the ice—that captivated Angela. By 1972 at age eight, she was playing on the Flemingdon Boy's House League Team and was the top scorer.

However, not everyone was happy that the top scorer was a girl. Although she had lots of friends who were boys, they weren't the problem. It was their fathers. Some of them didn't want a girl showing up their sons, so they demanded that Angela not be allowed to join the next year. In those days, people just couldn't imagine that girls could be better at sport than boys, and so Angela wasn't allowed to play.

Angela was hurt by those fathers' attitudes, and as she grew up she realized that sexism was a part of hockey. "As far as I can tell, hockey's like that. It's what you get used to. You adapt. It's the ones with the lesser ability who discriminate," she says.

After Angela wasn't allowed to play on the boys' team, she was told that she had to play with girls. Even though she was so much better than most female players and even though their games were far away, Angela kept playing. She and her mother, Donna, would gather up her hockey equipment and board the bus by their home. Her two sisters, Kim and Cindy, would tag along, so Angela had her own personal cheering section at her games. They found a team at Victoria Park Arena, which was half an hour away by bus.

"When I arrived, some of the players were skating in figure skates," says Angela. "There was no consistency, anyone could play from all ages and abilities. It wasn't like boys' hockey where people were divided up by ability and age."

Sometimes the trips to other hockey arenas took

two hours, because the teams were so scattered and given the worst ice-time. In those days most girls' teams didn't have home ice; they had to use whatever arena had a spare hour when the boys' teams weren't playing. This is why the games were held some distance apart, and girls had to play and practise at late hours, which is dangerous. The outside of most hockey arenas is not well lit; the rinks are often isolated and in less safe parts of the city. Still, Angela persevered and outscored all the other girls in Metro Toronto.

In 1978, at age fourteen, she graduated to a senior women's team called the Toronto Islanders. She was the youngest player on the team, and playing against women in their twenties and thirties. By the time she was seventeen, Angela had made the Central Ontario All-Star Team—something she would do for the next twenty-three years, until retirement. (The All-Star Team doesn't necessarily play, but it is an honour to be named to the team, which recognizes the best players in the league each year.) Angela spent six years as the Central Ontario League's top scorer, and three as the MVP, and was a constant on the Ontario team to the Canadian championships, where she picked up more MVP awards as she regularly outscored players from all the other provinces.

I.D.E.A.S. PHOTOGRAPHY

Like other female players across Canada, Angela had dreams that went beyond the country's borders. She wanted to see how she stacked up against the best players in the world, but there weren't any international tournaments. There had been a national team for men for decades, and the National Hockey League (NHL), but nothing for women. And yet Canadian women's hockey has such a rich history.

The first photograph of a game of hockey played by women was taken at the Governor General's home in Ottawa in 1891, when Lady Stanley, the wife of the Governor General, hosted a game. In 1894, women at Queen's University formed a team against the wishes of the Anglican archbishop, and by 1921 the University of Toronto had defeated McGill at the university championships.

Unfortunately, most of the gains made by women on the ice rink in the first part of the century were wiped out during the late 1940s and into the 1960s, until the Women's Movement came along. It was because so many women demanded equality in this time period, that girls like Angela were able to have any ice-time at all, even if it was difficult to obtain. Things were not equal yet, so women continued to fight for their right to play. In 1967, the first Dominion Ladies Hockey Tournament was held and 22 teams competed. Thirty years later, 400 Canadian teams competed.

While she was a student, Angela had to be patient and do what she could to fulfill her dreams. After high school, she enrolled in the Seneca College sports administration course in Toronto and organized and coached at several hockey camps. Girls and women from all over clamoured to attend an Angela James hockey camp. When she graduated in 1985, Angela became a College employee and ran the recreation program there. She also started her own Breakaway Hockey School, which she ran out of the College in the summertime.

Finally in 1987 Angela and other top Canadian players got a break. It was announced that Canada would host the first world tournament for women's hockey in Ottawa. It wasn't an official world championship, but it was a start. Angela tried out, along with Canada's best female players from across the country. She proved to be outstanding.

Eight countries, including Finland, Sweden, the United States, and Japan, attended, and so did thousands of fans. While it was the first time female hockey players could play internationally, the women's team was not allowed to wear the same national team uniform as the men's. Instead, they were made to wear pink jerseys and white shorts—as if they were "little sisters" to the men's national team. Still, this tournament was a great start. The Canadian women's team handily won the tournament and Angela was voted MVP overall.

This first world tournament created plenty of new opportunities. In 1990, the International Ice Hockey Federation (IIHF) agreed to the first ever official World Championships for women. Ottawa played host again, and a Canadian women's national team to the World Championships had to be chosen. Despite Angela's great showing in Ottawa three years earlier, the Canadian Hockey Association (CHA) didn't want to name her to the team. According to the coach at the time, the late Dave McMaster, the CHA had said that Angela and two other Toronto-based players had "an attitude problem." (One of the other players they didn't want to name to the team was Geraldine Heaney, who ended up playing on every national team from the 1987 tournament to the 2002 Olympics when the women won gold.) These two women had been pioneers in the game. Although the CHA never said why they didn't immediately name Angela to the team, it seems that they weren't ready for this new assertiveness.

However Dave McMaster wasn't going to let a star like Angela sit on the sidelines. He had a tournament to win. Coach McMaster told the CHA it was crazy to name a national team and not include Angela James and Geraldine Heaney. The women had good reason to be confident: they were two of the best players in the world. "Angela was the best," said Coach McMaster just weeks before he passed away in 2003. "She would be dominant on the ice—quite simply, she was the top player. What were they trying to do by withholding her name until later? It was ridiculous."

Angela did play in that tournament and Coach McMaster's prediction was right. She did dominate. Angela scored the first goal at the first Women's World Hockey Championship. Later she told television cameras, "We're doing this for the little girls who are coming up." She ended up getting a hat-trick (three goals) in that game and was named to the World All-Star Team after the championships wound up.

After that, women's hockey started to gain momentum. In 1992 Finland hosted the World Championships and Angela once again dominated, and once again was named to the World All-Star Team. In 1994 she was named Best Forward at the World Championships, but she wasn't just playing hockey during this time, she was coaching too. On top of her summer hockey school, Angela coached the senior women's AA Toronto Red Wings, and was an advisory coach for the AA Newtonbrook Panthers. She continued to make every national team that went to the World Championships, and that team won the gold every time. "Skate" was practically Angela's middle name. With four and a half weeks of holidays, and another three weeks of lieu time, Angela used every spare day off work for hockey. She never took a "vacation."

But in 1998 another opportunity was created. After so many successful women's world championships, the IIHF agreed to allow women's hockey in the Olympics. Angela was overjoyed. To play at the Olympics had been her dream since she was a little girl. Even though she lived in Toronto and had a full-time job there, she took a leave of absence from work when she was invited to train for six months full time before the Olympics. She made a commitment to the Canadian team and moved to Calgary in the fall of 1997 so she could train at hockey's national headquarters. "When they first announced that women's hockey would be in the Olympics, I definitely wanted to be a part of it," said Angela just before she moved. "I think the attitudes of the public and the media have really changed. People who didn't know about women's hockey started to get interested."

Since 1988, when Calgary hosted the Winter Olympics, athletes have gone to that city to train at the state-of-the-art facilities. One of the benefits of training in Calgary is that it is approximately 450 metres (1,500 feet) above sea level. Being higher than sea level is thought to be good for athletes when they are training, as there is less oxygen in the air. Less oxygen forces the body to produce more red blood cells. Red blood cells carry oxygen to the muscles, so the more red blood cells athletes have, the more oxygen is in their body. Athletes need more oxygen when they play for long periods of time. And when they return to places with lower altitudes, they benefit from having more oxygen-carrying red blood cells in their body.

However, when Angela got to Calgary, she felt dizzy and had trouble sleeping. Well, she thought,

I am at a higher altitude now, so that may cause dizziness, and the workouts are tough, so maybe that's why I am losing weight, feeling light-headed, and having problems sleeping.

Twenty-five players were invited to the six-month-long training camp, but only twenty would make the Olympic team. There was tension. People had been friends before this, but now they eyed each other warily. Who was going to be cut from the team? The head coach, Shannon Miller, put the players through plenty of gruelling workouts. They didn't just train on the ice. They worked out in the weight room and went running and cycling. Exercise physiologists, people who study how to move the body efficiently when it is doing activity like skating, worked with the team to help them perfect every motion they used in the game. Nutritionists worked with them so they would eat healthy foods that could help fuel them on the ice. Preparing for the Olympics is a lot of hard work.

As people watched the team prepare, some thought that Angela had lost some of her zip on the ice. They didn't think the old Angela was out there, skating quickly with the puck and being aggressive with other players. Where was the spark? At an international tournament in December, Shannon decided to send out a younger player and sat Angela on the bench.

Angela James on the bench? No one had seen this before. Angela watched the game, which Canada lost, in stony silence.

Shannon had cut all the extra players except one by this tournament, and no matter how much she wanted to bring everyone to the Olympics, international rules would only allow her to bring twenty players. She asked Angela to come to her office. It was the most difficult thing Shannon ever had to do. She told Angela that she had believed, until recently, that Angela was one of the best female players in the world. But Angela was not playing well enough to win a gold medal for Canada at the Olympics, and it was Shannon's job as coach to bring that medal home. She told Angela she had not made the Olympic team.

Angela at first thought that she hadn't heard her coach properly. It had been her dream since she played on the roads of Flemingdon Park to be an Olympic hockey player. She felt whatever was wrong with her was only temporary. She'd gain back the weight she'd lost in time for the Olympics. Besides which, she didn't believe her lower body weight had affected her game in the first place.

But Angela *had* heard correctly. She had to leave the camp that day, and so all alone, she packed her things, piled them into her little car, and drove across the frozen prairies, back home to Toronto. "It was like a searing arrow through my heart," said Angela later. "You couldn't have hurt me in any worse way."

Back home, the dizziness didn't go away. Angela started feeling much worse. Finally she went to the doctor. There were a lot of tests done and when they came back, she found out she had Graves' Disease, a symptom of which was hyper-thyroidism. A person's thyroid, which is a gland in the neck, is responsible for how quickly or slowly we burn calories. If the thyroid becomes "hyper" it works overtime, and burns more calories than it should. This is why Angela was losing weight and feeling tired.

Angela was treated for her disease, and her body responded, but her spirit was nearly broken. She couldn't even watch the Olympics, but when some of her friends heard that the Canadian team won silver instead of gold, they believed it was because Angela wasn't in the lineup. "Of course they didn't win gold," said Cathy Phillips after the Olympics. Cathy was the goalie on the first Canadian women's teams, and an old pal of Angela's. "If they send a rookie out on the ice in the final game, the Americans say, 'Oh good, a rookie.' If they had sent Angela out on the ice, they would have said, 'Uh-oh, it's Angela James.'"

But as much as Angela felt that arrow of disappointment pierce her heart, she believed she still had a life to live, and she had to become as healthy as possible. She had a point to prove to the Canadian public. In the summer of 1998 she was training hard again in the weight room at the Ice Gardens at York University with her long-time friend and teammate Geraldine Heaney. By this time, Angela was playing for the Toronto Aeros, a top team in the National Women's Hockey League, the NWHL. Angela had decided she was going to make it back onto the Canadian team. She was still on medication for her illness, but she was gaining weight and felt great.

By the 1998–99 season, Angela was at the top of the scoring and assists list for the NWHL. In the fall of 1999 she was selected to play for the Canadian national team at the Three Nations Cup in Montreal, where she scored the final goal in the deciding game. After this, Angela retired on her own terms from the national team, though she still played for the Aeros, who became the Beatrice Aeros in 1999 when the dairy company stepped in and generously helped the team out. Angela knew she had proven she could come back and play at the top international level, but she didn't want to risk another run-in with the CHA. She felt satisfied with knowing she could play with the best in the world, and gracefully bowed out of world play.

Angela went back to running the recreation program at Seneca College, and coaching at her hockey school, as well as for the Junior Aeros team. Girls continued to come out in droves when she was behind the bench. By the 2003–04 season, she had also taken her four levels of officiating hockey, which made it possible for her to ref at the international level. "I think I've finished with coaching at the club level for now," says Angela. "I reffed the CISS (Canadian Interuniversity Sport) last year. I'd be interested in coaching in the university scene at some point," she adds, "but I have a four-year-old boy, and he's my main priority now. He was two months old at the Three Nations Cup, and I don't want to be all over the place when he's young."

Angela says in life and in sports girls should "do whatever's best for them to achieve their dreams.

Figure it out for yourself. Nothing is perfect and there will always be problems. But when I look at the positive experiences and compare them with the negative ones in hockey, definitely there were many more good times."

Sonia Denoncourt:
Kicking Down Barriers

"I started playing soccer when I was nine," says Sonia Denoncourt, "and I loved it from the start." Sonia is the first woman in the world to become an international referee. And she made the jump from player to official when she was still a teenager. At fourteen years of age she was the captain of her soccer team in Sherbrooke, Quebec, and her coach asked her one day to try refereeing. Sonia wasn't sure she knew how, but he insisted she try. He told her she was a natural leader, already the captain of the team, and would be well suited for officiating. "I played soccer for another six years and also reffed during that time," says Sonia. "It was the beginning of my career. I started out on a field in Sherbrooke, Quebec, and now I travel the world."

Sonia was born in 1964 and she still looks like a top athlete. She believes that in order to run and follow the ball, and still be able to make proper calls in soccer, a ref has to be in top condition. She trains hard for her international reffing position with the Fédération Internationale de Football Association (FIFA), the international football soccer federation. It's a long journey from the days when she was still a teenager and making calls against players much older than her. "I was lucky, I think," says Sonia, "because when I was young, I didn't have a lot of coaches and parents yelling at me, and I understand other young refs are intimidated more today. Now that soccer has become more popular, many coaches and parents think a fourteen and under game is a World Cup final. When I finally did meet people who intimidated me, I was prepared for them. I had a toolbox of experience by then."

Sonia had two dreams for a long time. Becoming really successful in soccer was one, and becoming a physical education teacher was another. The two dreams started to come together in university. By then she had been officiating for five years, and she enrolled in the phys. ed. department of the Université de Sherbrooke in Quebec. While still reffing, Sonia continued her education at the Université d'Ottawa, where she took a master's degree in Sport Administration. At the same time, she enrolled in courses in coaching and officiating, and was also able to teach phys. ed. "My dreams came true," she says. "I'm very lucky."

DALE MACMILLAN / CSA

Sonia, in the middle, with two of her colleagues

Soon she had the ability to ref national level games and for ten years worked in the men's A League, which is a First Division professional league in Canada. "It was quite demanding," Sonia notes. "I had to pass the men's physical fitness test, and there were plenty of hard plays to mediate. It took a lot of mental concentration."

In those days women's soccer at the university level and club level wasn't nearly as big as it is now. There were no university national championships for women, nor were there any Olympic games for women, but there were for men. It was women like Sonia who worked hard to change this situation. Now Canadian university soccer for women is huge, and women's soccer had its inaugural Olympics in 1996 at the Atlanta Games.

Even though women have made progress, however, there's still a great deal of work that needs to be done. There aren't many women involved with international soccer, let alone working as referees. Right now FIFA has twenty-six people on its executive committee. This committee makes all the important decisions about soccer for the world, including who gets to be a referee. Only one member is female.

So how did Sonia manage to become the first woman to referee international soccer when she has to work with an organization that has allowed so few women in it? She combines hard work, lots of brains, talent, and an understanding of the game that stops many men in their tracks. As well, the Canadian government made a commitment to improving sport for women and girls. Starting in the early 1980s, Sport Canada, the organization responsible for national sport in Canada, began to see how few women there were in decision-making positions. They decided they would have to create opportunities for women to move up the ladder in sports.

"In Canada we held a national female symposium in soccer," says Sonia. "For four days, twenty-seven people in soccer met and looked at game analysis, and learned how to make calls in games that are played at a high level. We also created a mentor system so women could help women."

At the same time that Sonia was learning how to ref national-level games, girls and women were taking to the game in unprecedented numbers. Cities and towns all over Canada have had to open up their pitches to women and girls as they lace up cleats and start dribbling to their heart's content. In 2002, there were 307,258 registered female players with the Canadian Soccer Association. That is 31,866 more players than in 2001. And the numbers keep growing. The CSA had 342,976 registered female players in 2003. Sonia was part of this big change in her sport. Even though World Cup and Olympic events had been held for male soccer players for decades, the first women's world championship wasn't held until 1988. China hosted this competition and there were no female officials. In 1991, China also hosted the first women's World Cup. This time three or four women assisted, but none was a referee.

In 1994 Sonia made sport history by successfully passing the test to referee internationally. She was the only fully qualified female ref, but four other women had passed the test to be international assistant refs. By then Sonia had been reffing for twelve years. Women could finally make decisions about a women's game. Soon after she became an international ref, Linda Black of

New Zealand joined her. Now there were two qualified women, and more would follow. In 1995, FIFA put together a men's list of refs and a women's list. This way, contests that involved women's teams could hire female refs. Sweden hosted the women's World Cup that year and twelve out of thirty-two refs were women. And at the Summer Olympics in Atlanta in 1996, when women's soccer was first added, the entire tournament was officiated by women. By the time the United States hosted the women's World Cup in 1999, there was a pool of refs to choose from.

"Every year we increased the amount of women officiating internationally," says Sonia. "Now there are over 100 of us." This is the fairest way to officiate, as the refs should be from countries that don't have a stake in the outcome of the game. At the Under 19 World Cup in Edmonton in August 2002, there were twenty-four refs: twelve chief refs, and twelve assistant refs. One hundred percent were female and from all over the world. It was the first time any of them had officiated at the international level. After that, they can ref senior World Cup events.

Sonia says a good official must have courage and patience, and be physically and mentally fit because of the high demands of the job. There is a great deal of work managing emotions on the soccer field, which makes reffing difficult sometimes. And it's not always the players who are emotional. Coaches and officials can lose their cool too. It's important to remember that everyone brings a different set of attitudes to the soccer pitch. "We all have different social beliefs, and different backgrounds," she says, "especially in international play. But there is a set of laws for soccer, and the difference between a good official and an excellent official is the management of the laws."

So how does a ref manage the laws of soccer? Sonia says the number one rule is, no matter how hot-headed everyone else gets, the ref keeps cool. In her twenty-five years of officiating she has never once lost her temper. "You have nothing to gain by getting excited," she advises. "My rule is, every time they raise their voice, I lower mine. Sometimes it's better to say nothing at all. Sometimes I just say 'enough' and get back to the game. Refs absolutely never get involved in fights. We try to prevent them by physically trying to get between players so they can't get at one another. But if a fight starts we will take notes and decide on the penalty later." Fights rarely happen in soccer, and are even more rare in women's soccer than men's.

Refs are never to touch a player, though Sonia says the only exception to this is when a player is on the ground. It is considered a sign of good sportswomanship to help them get up, but no comments such as “nice play” or “good goal” can be made because refs must be neutral if they are to do their jobs properly. Sonia says she believes the players know she has a lot of respect for them and for the game, and this comes from years of being an alert but fair-minded official.

But all the fairness in the world won’t help a ref who can’t keep up with the play, and this is why they have to be in such good shape. Sonia’s exercise regimen is nearly as tough as the players’. She trains five to six days a week, and while reffing at the World Cup, each official must do at least two hours of training every morning. FIFA hired a full-time trainer for them at the 2003 World Cup. They did one hour of technical work such as running sideways, backwards, then forwards, as if they were reffing a game. This would be followed by fitness training for endurance, which meant they would go for a long run, swim, or work out on a stationary bike or rowing machine. To be a FIFA official, they have to have a medical exam every year, and then another one before they ref at a big tournament. Added to this is a fitness test they do three times a year that includes two 50-metre sprints, two 100-metre sprints, a couple of minutes' break and then a 12-minute run in which they must cover at least 2,700 metres. They must pass this test again before they are allowed to officiate at a World Cup. But those are just standards for the basic fitness skills. Once the ref hits the soccer pitch there are other skills involved. "We must always be aware of the angle of our vision when we are running," Sonia says. "You must be able to run and be able to watch the game with intensity. You also have to make sure you are running in a direction that won't impede the play, so you must watch out for the players and the ball."

DALE MACMILLAN / CSA

To those outside soccer, her regime seems incredible. In each game the average ref runs 12 to 15 kilometres, and usually there is an average of 500 decisions being made per game. The toughest decisions are the penalty calls, says Sonia, because a penalty kick may determine the outcome of the game. “Carding” players is also a difficult call for refs. Usually, she says, bad behaviour by a player will result in a verbal warning, but if a player goes a little beyond this behaviour again, or does something worse, she will receive a yellow card. If she receives another one in the same game, then she is ejected. If her behaviour is really bad, there will be no verbal warnings or yellow cards. She will receive a red card and be ejected immediately. Her coach will not be allowed to replace her and the team must play for the rest of the game without that position.

Sonia also works full time for the Canadian Soccer Association (CSA) as a director of officials. They are the perfect employer to have, since she can always get time off to ref an international event. Sonia says the situation works well for her: the CSA is good to her when she's home, and FIFA takes care of her when she is on the road. She was away for thirty-one days while reffing at the World Cup in the fall of 2003, and grocery shopping, cooking, and housework was taken care of by FIFA. In return, they expect the refs to be extremely good at what they do, with no excuses for mistakes.

There's a lot of pressure on officials at World Cups because soccer is by far the most popular sport in the world, and sometimes calls are very hard to make. "Every game I've officiated has had hard calls," Sonia says. "It doesn't matter if it's a local game or a World Cup final, there are three tests of whether or not I won. The first is, Did I feel good about the game? The second is, Do I feel I did the best I could do? And third is, Did I give the players the respect they deserve?" Sonia may be on the international stage when reffing for FIFA, but she takes local games seriously too. All players are equal in her eyes.

At the 2003 World Cup in the United States, Sonia was one of thirty-six female referees, and was one of four refs chosen to ref the final game between Sweden and Germany. At the end of the tournament, Sonia had officiated at three World Cups in a row, and two consecutive Olympics. In total, she has officiated for twenty-six years and has been a ref with FIFA since 1994. No ref in the history of soccer anywhere in the world, whether male or female, has matched Sonia's record of consistency and dedication. She has ninety caps—when a player or ref is "capped" it means she has made an appearance at an international event. No ref has matched her in reffing ninety international games either.

"I've seen such changes over the years. I love it," she says. "Every single game I ref is a challenge. This is a very demanding sport, physically and mentally. But I like to run, and I like to travel. I'm paid to do this. I think after all these years I have seen every trick on the field. Still there's never a game the same. It gives me great satisfaction."

To operate in her whirlwind international world of sport, Sonia speaks English and French fluently, and "gets by" in Spanish. If girls have dreams of an international career, she strongly suggests they learn more than one language. And what else does she advise? "Make sure you have a good balance in your life, if you want to be successful. Try not to forget your family and friends. You need a lot of discipline to do all of this. You have to be willing to commit and get involved with your life. At the same time, you need support too. You can't break barriers without support, so don't stay with people who don't give it to you.

"Every detail matters. Think about the way you dress, the way you talk, the way you treat players. Always have respect and eventually you will receive it back.

"For some of us, this took a long time. Women still don't get that much in comparison to men. The media needs to change. Women's sport is not respected. It's still a battle. It's slightly better, but we are still far behind. Internationally, women are still neglected."

Women and girls don't have equality in sports yet. But with pioneers like Sonia leading the way, perhaps our daughters or granddaughters will. And what better place to start than the playing field? We can have fun, and work towards a world that includes everyone.

Kendra Ohama:
Wheeling and Shooting Her Way Around the World

Kendra always loved sports, but it wasn't until she found out how exciting wheelchair basketball was that she took herself seriously as an athlete. One day she was shopping, and a man—who would later become her coach—came up to her and asked if she would be interested in playing wheelchair basketball. It took her by surprise, but he told her they were practising at Calgary General Hospital, and she decided to see what the sport was about.

"It was the first time I had been in a chair that was so movable and I thought, 'Wow, this is great! I'm going to use this as an everyday chair.' I had so much coordination to wheel and dribble." So began Kendra's amazing career in wheelchair basketball, though the journey towards her career had started many years earlier.

Kendra's family had a potato farm near Ranier, Alberta, a small town outside Calgary, and like most farm kids, the six children in her family all had plenty of chores. They would have to grade potatoes, make sure the sprinkler was running

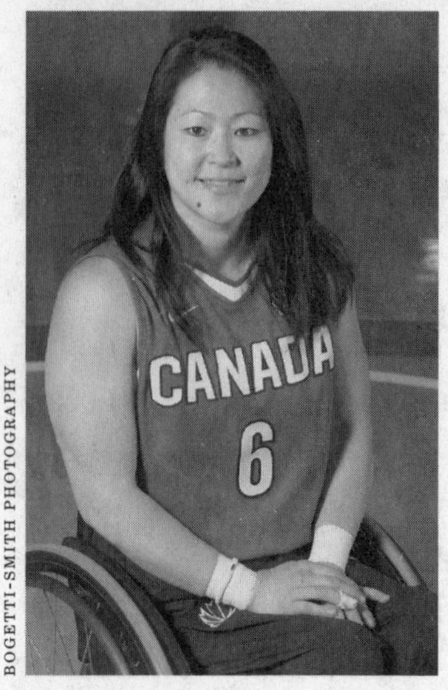

BOGETTI-SMITH PHOTOGRAPHY

properly, and sometimes even change the sprinkler's pipes. Everyone worked hard, but her family had always worked hard. Kendra's grandparents had come to Canada from Japan, but still had family and friends there. During harvest time, Japanese friends of the family would make the long trip to Canada and help out. Kendra and her siblings were young at the time, and they didn't grow up speaking Japanese and couldn't communicate too well with their visitors.

Kendra says both her mom and dad were born in Canada and they ran into racism when they were kids. "Our parents didn't want us to learn Japanese," she says. "They had a hard time when they were growing up and so they wanted us to fit in. Unfortunately I didn't learn the language. Except," she says with a laugh, "all the bad words." Years later in her career as an international athlete, Kendra realized how much she would have loved to speak Japanese.

In Ranier, even though she had plenty of chores at home, Kendra played many sports at school. Because she often stayed late to practise, when she was a teenager, she would sometimes drive to school instead of taking the school bus. One winter day while Kendra was in high school, she was driving to school when she hit black ice. The car spun out of control and Kendra flew out the windshield. "I was a typical sixteen-year-old," she comments. "I thought seat belts were for other people.

"Just after the accident when they flew me to Foothills Hospital, I was in and out of consciousness, but I remember asking the doctor if I was ever going to walk again," she says. "I think that may have helped me, that my subconscious was already trying to accept that I wouldn't walk again."

Indeed, her doctor told her she wouldn't walk, but her physiotherapist thought she could, and they set about to see if this was possible. With the help of many months of strenuous exercise and practice, Kendra was able to walk with braces from her feet to her hips, and a set of crutches. Her physiotherapist told her it was thanks to her healthy active body that she was able to make quick and amazing progress in her rehabilitation. Kendra had always loved volleyball, baseball, badminton, and participated in judo and track and field too. "My doctor came in and he was really surprised. But I thought the braces were too slow and I had to use both hands with the crutches, so I decided to use a chair." Kendra was so intent on learning how to go with the flow of her new life that she thinks that is why she didn't experience any depression. And she began to realize how important her sports background was.

Five years later she showed up at Calgary General Hospital and started to play basketball—the one sport she hadn't played seriously in high school. At first she played with the Calgary Grizzlies, which was a men's team that wanted to see more women playing. These men believed that everyone belonged on the basketball court, and they weren't keen on seeing another sport develop that seemed to be mainly for men. Before long, six to eight women started showing up for practices, and Kendra's first women's team, the Rocky Mountain Rollers, started to gel. What was really interesting to Kendra was that at first, she was the only person who actually used a wheelchair off the court. "Everyone else was able-bodied who just liked playing wheelchair basketball. The chair is seen as part of your equipment, not as a sign of disability."

As sport for the disabled started to gain popularity in the late 1980s, able-bodied people started trying out activities like wheelchair basketball and realized they really enjoyed the challenge. Kendra says there's lots of debate over who should play and compete in wheelchair sports. There are many, like her original teammates in Calgary, who believe that wheelchairs are no different than basketballs—they are equipment used to play a game. Some people will stand up and get out of them at the end of the game, and some people will stay in theirs and use them for transportation. Others believe that there aren't enough opportunities for disabled people as it is, especially women and girls, and so all available positions should go to them. But even among disabled athletes there are a variety of abilities.

"There are different class systems in disabled sport," explains Kendra, "depending on where the spinal cord is injured, or what else may have put you in a wheelchair, like having a leg amputated or having spina bifida. If you are a high-functioning paraplegic," she continues, "you will have use of your abdominal muscles, which will give you an advantage over someone whose injury is lower."

Kendra is a high-functioning paraplegic. She has seven straps that hold her onto her chair when she plays: two on her feet, three at the knees, one at the hips, and one around her waist. "I never come loose from my chair," she says. "When the chair falls, so do I." But Kendra's also good at getting right back into the game, and points out that chairs take most of the damage in falls. The straps help her so she "can manipulate and push and wiggle my hips a little and I'll move. I can lean forward too and receive the ball from the side, and bring the ball in to my hips."

After that first workout, Kendra knew she'd found her sport. She dedicated herself to being the best she could possibly be. "I went all summer and winter to the gym," she says. "I didn't miss a practice and I trained with the men's and women's teams. We played in Edmonton and in the United States. I did a lot of wheeling too—10 kilometres, three times a week."

In the summer of 1990 Kendra was invited to her first national team camp in Vancouver, as a guard. She didn't make the team, but the experience was really important for her because she learned what skills she had to work on. She came home and worked on the accuracy of her shot, and on rebounds. Kendra trained as hard as she could for the next ten months, because if she made the team in 1991, she knew she'd have a good shot at making the team competing in 1992 at the Barcelona Paralympic Games. All her efforts paid off and Kendra played on the team that went to the World Stoke–Mandeville International Tournament in England. Canada took the gold at that tournament over ten teams, and started on a gold medal roll that would continue for more than ten years.

By winning at the Stoke–Mandeville Tournament, the Canadian team had qualified for the Paralympic Games. But individual players still had to qualify for that team. In Canada, players still have to try out each year for the national team, even if they were world champions the year before. The team wouldn't be announced until the summer of 1992. There was another year of training and flying out to Vancouver to train with the national coach, Tim Frick, at Douglas College, where he coached the able-bodied varsity basketball team. Finally, though, after much hard work and sweat, Kendra heard the magic words she had waited for all year. She had made the team that was going to Barcelona.

"My experiences in Spain were the most memorable of my life, partly because these were my first Games and I'd never been to a competition like this before. But there were so many other things too," adds Kendra. "The food was so exotic and we were right on the Mediterranean in a building with a ramp that was built especially for us to wheel right down to the beach.

"But it wasn't until we started playing that it really hit me—the crowds were thunderous. In the final against the U.S. we couldn't hear each other because the fans were going so crazy." At the end of that game, the Canadian team won gold. Kendra felt like she was dreaming.

Four years later the team won the gold medal again in Atlanta, Georgia, at the Paralympic Games there, but their off-court experience wasn't nearly as nice. "This time the food was awful and they stuffed us into these little apartments. You couldn't turn your chair around to get into the bathroom without opening the front door. One day the transportation people forgot about us completely and we waited for two hours after a game to be picked up.

"There was a decent crowd for the final against the Netherlands," she adds, "but we went to the closing ceremonies after that and it was a nightmare. There was no organization and just a few buses, and all the able-bodied people went in front of us and took all the spaces in the buses. It was terrible."

Those bad memories of Atlanta didn't daunt the

team, though. They trained harder than ever for the next four years and went off to Sydney, Australia, as the favourites. "The crowds were fabulous there," says Kendra. "They love their sports so much, we ended up beating the United States by a big margin in the final, and everyone in the stands went nuts. Off the court we went downtown, or travelled wherever we wanted. People were so friendly."

Kendra says one of the reasons the team has done so well for so many years is their mental training. Players from other countries may be faster or have better skills, and the U.S. athletes are much younger, most of them in their mid-twenties. The Canadians, meanwhile, are in their mid-thirties, but they visualize and imagine different scenarios—at the foul line, in layups, everything. In their imaginations they add all the distractions, the fans, the refs, the bad calls, anything that might make them overlook their task and take their focus off the moment. They just won't allow outside distractions to bother them.

"For all athletes, you have to know your routine before the game. Same thing goes with off the court," says Kendra. "You have to organize your personal life so you can focus on your sport and not worry too much about personal problems.

They seem to melt away when you focus on the positive things.

"The other thing is, if you get too involved in personal problems, it will affect team cohesion. Our team gets along really well, and we respect our coach."

In the summer of 2002, the team's winning streak since 1991 was finally broken by the U.S. at a tournament in Brazil, but they only let it happen once. They arrived in Kitakyūshū, Japan, for the World Championships that fall, determined to get their streak back, and they did. But it wasn't winning the World Crown that most affected Kendra this time. It was visiting Japan, the country of her ancestors.

During these World Championships, the Canadian women were becoming superstars. They won game after game, eventually capturing yet another gold medal. Fans loved them, and with their bright red and white jackets and track pants, the team could go few places without being celebrities.

"After one game I received a message that somebody was coming over to meet me. The team went down to dinner, and afterwards I noticed a couple were waiting near us. The man had worked for my parents all those years ago and he and his wife drove two hours just to see me. I was so moved by this. I don't know how they found out, but they knew I was playing on the Canadian team all these years later."

After the final game, while Kendra celebrated in the change room with her teammates and took her time getting out to the stadium lobby, another family was waiting to see her. Yet another young man who had worked for her parents when he was in his teens had tracked her down. He brought his wife and daughter along to meet her.

"His little girl had brought flowers for me. I was overwhelmed that they would wait so long to say hello. I wish I had known they were waiting and I wouldn't have celebrated for so long in the change room.

"It was weird and exciting to be in Japan. I never expected it to be that way. I still see myself as a Canadian, but I felt like I had come home. Our coach sent me out to play at the end of the final, and he had tears in his eyes. He said, 'This one's for Gonzo'—that's my nickname. I realized he was crying because I was playing in the place of my heritage."

But there was even more soul searching for Kendra in Japan. She found a piece of history there that has made her study the country in a much more detailed way. "I went to Hiroshima, and I was overwhelmed there too. I had heard about the bomb being dropped, but you can't imagine what the people must have gone through. It's so surreal when you think about some of the things that happen—it's your own heritage, not just history."

"I wasn't expecting to have that connection at all," says Kendra. "I'm not sure exactly what I was feeling. People just seemed to be drawn to me, just because I was Japanese, and there I was, not understanding a word of what they were saying! I wish my parents had taught us the language, but I know they thought they were speaking English for our own good."

Kendra looks towards the Paralympic Games in Athens, Greece, in September 2004 as her next big challenge. Today Canada has a junior women's wheelchair basketball team, and Kendra says there are around five players who are starting to push for spots on the senior team, so she's training hard to maintain her position, and preparing for setbacks. It's been a long journey from the accident in Ranier, to the Grizzlies, to the Rocky Mountain Rollers, to her World Championship golds and three Paralympic victories. Athens will be another big step in Kendra's journey.

"I keep hearing stories that everything is behind schedule," she says. "We coped well with what happened in Atlanta when we were left behind after the game, but hopefully that won't happen there. I think it's going to be cool to play in the home of the ancient Olympic games. To be able to say, 'This is where the Olympic running races began' would be great. To be a part of that history makes me feel very lucky and fortunate—that is, as long as I make the team."

Anne Breaks:
Second Star on the Right and Straight on Till Morning

Usually the only time we hear about female athletes in the media is when they have won an Olympic or World Championship medal. There are a few of those athletes in this book too, but most athletes—male or female—don't make it to the Olympics, and many don't aspire to be world champions in the first place. Anne Breaks is one of those people. She loves her sports, but they are just one of the ways she is preparing for a different career of a lifetime. Since she was a little girl, Anne has dreamed of being an astronaut. Now that she is a young woman, sports, school, and a spirit inside her that wants to find out about the unknown are combining to make that dream a reality.

"When I was little we lived in the Rocky Mountains," said Anne as she was about to leave for NASA's summer space school in 2001. "There wasn't any light pollution out there and very little TV reception. Every evening my family would go for a walk. The night sky was very dark and the celestial stars and constellations were vivid. I remember, since I was three years old, I used to look up at the stars and wonder what it was like to be up there."

By eight years of age, Anne, who was born in 1985, was devouring and memorizing every book she could get her hands on from the local library about space exploration. She even joined a program of astronomy, math, and physics, and eventually, when she was fifteen years old, she wrote the Royal Astronomy Society's astronomy exam. She earned the highest score amongst those who wrote it the day she did. Anne was hooked on space.

After she did so well on the exam, Anne was the only young person invited to a conference at the University of Calgary's Institute of Space Research. There she met one of her big-time role models, Canadian astronaut Julie Payette.

Julie Payette was Canada's second woman in space, and Anne couldn't wait to talk to her. Julie told her that to be an astronaut she had to be many things, and an athlete was high on that list. Astronauts must have a high level of physical fitness to endure the changes that happen in the body while living in space. At the time Julie did her first space excursion, she was a competitive triathlete. She loved swimming, running, and

COURTESY ELAINE BREAKS

cycling, but also learned how to get through difficult and even painful situations by doing a sport that takes longer to complete than a marathon does. Sports taught her a lot about self-discipline and setting long-term goals. You don't become a good triathlete or astronaut overnight.

As well, Julie told Anne that your character is most important in space. Astronauts have to get along with people from other countries in a spaceship while they orbit the Earth. Who you were as a child will really count later on. Future astronauts need to pursue excellence in all of the skills they learn and not just try those skills on.

Anne too is a great lover of sports. Today she is training to take her red belt test in tae kwon do. If she is successful, the next level is her black-stripe belt, and then all she will have to earn is her final black belt. She is an advanced alpine skier and likes to Nordic ski as well. In the summer she loves to run and mountain bike, and she is a year-round swimmer with her bronze cross in life-guard training.

To make herself more familiar with the weightlessness one feels in space, she is working towards her PADI (Professional Association of Diving Instructors) scuba diving accreditation at the local dive shop in Calgary. Her scuba diving experience came in handy when Anne arrived at the Johnson Space Center in NASA in July 2001—she got to try out the Neutral Buoyancy Lab—a large pool that has a full-sized International Space Station and space shuttle immersed in 12 metres (40 feet) of water to simulate the working conditions in space. As Anne notes, "Newton's Laws of Physics change in space. For instance, we experience the laws of physics differently on Earth than in space because of gravity. His laws are far more apparent in space, and astronauts need to know this. Their every move and motion in space will be affected by physics. For example, on Earth if you are on in-line skates and you push off a wall, you will eventually roll to a stop because of friction and gravity. However, in space, if astronauts push off the side of the space station, friction will not make them stop moving. In fact, they will float off into space! We aren't used to zero gravity, so astronauts must train for it. The Neutral Buoyancy Lab helps astronauts become accustomed to the extreme effect of Newton's Laws in space."

Anne's three weeks at NASA were exciting. She stayed up until midnight absorbing information, and then got up again at 5 a.m. so she wouldn't miss anything. But when she returned to Calgary, she was once again Anne Breaks, sister of Jen, daughter of Elaine.

"It was the most amazing experience," says Anne of her three weeks at NASA. "We worked with astronauts, scientists—we even planned a mission. You really see how a team works. Every single person, from the person who sweeps the floor to the person in space, has a job to do and it matters to the entire mission that they do their part of the job correctly. So you have to be part of the team, but also know how to work independently and be reliable."

Anne was the "astronomer" on the Logistics Team at the space school in NASA. Her team had to simulate a plan for a spaceship's trip to Mars. She was even successful in coordinating a rocket's path to deflect a comet that was headed towards Earth in their mock voyage. She was able to navigate the Mars spacecraft using the planets as her reference points, and avoid the comet.

Becoming an astronaut is a tall order. While training herself physically to meet this challenge, however, Anne doesn't neglect other important aspects of her life. Astronauts need to be balanced, and to be able to communicate with their workmates, so she studies German at school and takes lessons in Russian as well. She plans on learning Japanese and who knows what other languages—because you never know who is going to end up in your spaceship. She plays the piano and is first flute in her school band, as well as playing for the Cadet band in Calgary, where she is a member of the 781 Air Cadets Squadron. She also has her amateur radio licence, to give her an idea of how short-wave radio works.

In the 2002–03 school year, Anne cut back a bit on her sports activities, though she still went to tae kwon do and took part in other physical activities. Her priority was school as she prepared to enter university. She was asked to attend universities all over the United States, and she also received a letter from Cambridge in England, but in the end she decided to go to the University of Calgary. They have a scholar's advantage program, which meant she could register early. One of the people she looks up to is Dr. Doug Hamilton. He's an alumnus of the University of Calgary and a flight surgeon at NASA. She wants to do her aerospace medical practicum with him after she makes it into medical school. Anne has finished her first year now in speech pathology, which she hopes will lead her to medical school.

The university is also connected to the Calgary Space Centre and is the home of the Institute of Space Research. Anne volunteered at the Institute in the summer before university, so she would be familiar with the Centre. She is also in demand internationally. She is the teen spokesperson for the international initiative called Space Day. It builds partnerships around the world that are dedicated to the exploration and understanding of space. In May 2003 she travelled to Washington, D.C., and met pioneer of space travel, astronaut John Glenn, and Sean O'Keefe, who is the head of NASA.

Meanwhile, the astronaut-in-training tries to balance that part of her personality with the role she plays as a member of the Breaks family.

Anne, her mother, and her sister are members of the Edgemont Club so they can work out together. Anne, at a fairly young age, has taken a path that will lead to her being away from her family, so she cherishes the time she can spend with them now. Anne is often asked to speak to the media and to schools, but when they can steal away for a few hours to lift weights, ride their bikes, or hike, they always do. Elaine is very proud of her daughter, and loves the time they can spend together in sports and physical activity because someday she knows Anne is more likely to be hurtling into space with an international crew. When kids who love space come over to visit, her mother thinks that something pretty cool starts to happen: the kids chat about their passion, but no one else has any idea what they're talking about. They understand science at a complex level. "But then we all go for a hike or a bike ride, and they're kids just horsing around. They have an indomitable spirit." When Anne's mom uses such a big word to describe her daughter and her friends, she means they have a spirit that can't get toppled over. No matter what challenges are put in front of them, they face them with an endless amount of energy.

Anne says girls should trust the spirit inside them that gives them the energy necessary to face challenges, but the fulfilment of these challenges and dreams may take many years, and can often be very difficult. “Don’t let anything stop you,” she says. “There’s still that stereotype of girls dancing and being all nice and frilly. I think this oppresses them. It makes you feel like your dreams are unrealistic.

“People think it’s weird if you go against what they think you should be,” Anne continues. “When I joined the Air Cadets because I wanted to be a pilot, the kids at school called me ‘Army Chick.’ I did things in Cadets like get really dirty when we trained and I was really physically fit. Those girls who teased me weren’t fit at all.

“I’m a good example of what can be accomplished.”

For Anne Breaks, the stars are the limit.

Justine Blainey:
Brave Trailblazer

Justine always wanted to play hockey. In the early 1980s her favourite player was Darryl Sittler of the Toronto Maple Leafs. "When I was six or seven, I kept asking my mom, 'I want to play hockey. I don't like tap dance, ballet, and figure skating.' And she said, 'No. Girls don't play hockey.'" Her brother, David, who is just eleven months younger than she is, was also a hockey fanatic. He was lobbying his mother so he could play as well.

"It took three years before my mom said, 'Okay, you've nagged enough. We'll find you a girls' team to play for,'" recalls Justine. After she played with a girls' team for a year, she knew she wanted to play with the guys. They had more competition, more hours of ice-time, the rinks were closer to her home, the games and practices were at better times, there was a more competitive atmosphere, and there were more tournaments.

When Justine turned twelve in 1985, she decided to play on the same team as her brother,

David, the Toronto Olympics team. "There was definitely a difference, and I wanted to be part of it. I wanted to be part of the highest level possible with people in my own age category," says Justine. "I finally said, 'Well, I want to play with the guys,' and male coaches said to me, 'Well, why don't you pretend you're a guy?' That wasn't for me. I did it for a while, but it wasn't my choice to pretend I was a boy. So eventually I had to fight for equality."

COURTESY DAVID BLAINEY

Justine tried out for a place on her brother's team, and made it. Now her mother, Caroline, would only have to drive to one set of practices and games. At least, that's what Justine thought.

But no sooner had she made the team than she was told she couldn't play because she was a girl. Her coach wanted her, but the Ontario Hockey Association (OHA) didn't, and the coach had to do what they said.

They just don't understand, thought Justine. I'll explain to the officials that I can play as well as my brother and they'll see that they made a mistake and let me play next week. But her mother wasn't so sure the "old boys" were going to let Justine play. She warned Justine that she was going to run into problems and asked her if she wanted to reconsider.

She thought Justine might get hurt, but in the end, she said, her daughter had argued the case well enough to win her over. It was now time to fight for Justine's right to play at the arena, and, if necessary, take the fight to court.

Justine's mother and brother were right behind her in her fight for equality, but Justine believes people thought it was her mother's idea. "People always feel that my mother was the pusher, the feminist, someone behind, pushing this little girl," she says. "She was the person who listened, and that's what I needed. I was a little girl who knew what she wanted. I was good enough, I made the team, and this was what I wanted to do. She supported me in those goals."

They hired a lawyer named Anna Fraser. She told them they would have to use the Canadian Charter of Rights and Freedoms to prove that

Justine had a right to play hockey on the team she had successfully tried out for. The year was 1985, and the Charter was very new.

The most crucial part of the Charter in Justine's battle was Section 15. This section is often called "the equality clause" because it recognizes that individuals are equal before and under the law, so they have the right to be protected by laws equally and benefit from them without discrimination. This includes discrimination based on race, national or ethnic origin, colour, religion, sex, age, or mental or physical disability.

Justine had to show that the Ontario Hockey Association had discriminated against her because of her sex, and therefore had violated the Charter. But the OHA had an ace up their sleeve. They said the Ontario Human Rights Code had its own section that made discrimination against girls in sport legal.

It's hard to believe that a human rights code would have a section that discriminated against girls, but in 1981, the province was changing its human rights code and men from sports organizations like the Ontario Hockey Association and the Ontario Softball Association told the government that sports would be contaminated if girls and boys played together, and that all the volunteer coaches, who were almost always men in those days, would quit. They refused to coach girls. The Ontario government believed the men, and added Section 19(2). This section said it wasn't against the law to discriminate against girls and women in sport and physical activity. When Justine came along, the OHA wasn't breaking any laws by not allowing her to play.

But Justine and her lawyer believed the Charter was a more important law than the Human Rights Code, and Justine was going to go to court to show that girls had every right to play with boys.

The fight was very long and painful. Justine's girlfriends at school turned against her. Almost her entire school—even many of her teachers—didn't support her. Justine was really hurt. She was only twelve years old and her friends had abandoned her. She would go to her locker and find awful things written on it. Justine had teachers not wanting to talk to her, and was told that she would have to repeat the year in school—and she had an 80-percent average—because she had missed too many classes going to court.

It is hard to imagine today, considering the fact we all cheered Hayley Wickenheiser on when she played on a professional men's team, that not very long ago the idea of girls and boys playing together made people so angry they would even commit acts of violence. People actually threatened to kill Justine. They wrote terrible letters to her telling her she would die. One man told her she was "the girl who wanted to destroy hockey" and pushed her down subway stairs in Toronto. Like tens of thousands of Canadian girls today, Justine was a polite, smart girl who also played hockey well. She just wanted to play on the same team as her brother at a time when hockey officials did not believe in equality.

Justine stuck it out at school, and argued that she would not repeat her year. She was in French immersion and, despite the time away from classes, graduated with a 97-percent average. While she was an extraordinary student, her friends never did come around. They shunned her, as did many women and girls in hockey for years to come. These are experiences Justine will never forget because they hurt her so much.

It took nearly three years, but Justine won. First of all, in the summer of 1986 the Supreme Court of Canada said they wouldn't hear the OHA's arguments. The OHA was trying to argue that it would hurt girls all over Canada if Justine played with boys. The problem was, there was no evidence to show that this was true. But the OHA didn't give up. Justine still had to go to the Human Rights Commission and prove that she should be allowed to play with boys. Justine had practised at hockey camps, but while she fought in the courts, the OHA passed a new rule not allowing anyone on the ice who wasn't on the team, so after that, she couldn't even practise. The Ontario Women's Hockey Association passed a petition around (and received many signatures) that would have Justine banned for life from women's hockey.

Justine had to wait until the following year before her case was heard at the Ontario Human Rights Commission. The lawyers for the OHA said that girls would be injured if they played with boys, that they didn't have the strength to hold their place on the ice or have enough speed to skate quickly with the puck.

Justine's lawyers (by now she needed more than Anna Fraser because the case was so big) had many experts. Two were women who had played hockey and then became sports medicine doctors and worked with hockey players. They said there was no evidence anywhere that showed that girls got hurt more than boys in sports.

The lawyer for the Human Rights Commission, Michael Bader, says he felt their job was to show the Commission that the measuring stick used to choose a team has nothing to do with whether a person is a boy or a girl, but whether they can play well. It is the coach choosing the team who decides this, and Justine's coach chose her because she did play well, especially on defence. The coach also liked that the more she played, the better she got. He didn't care whether she was a boy, a girl, or a mongoose. All he cared about was that she was the right hockey player for the team.

The OHA tried to use a lot of other arguments against Justine, but the experts and lawyers on her side always showed that they were wrong. Finally, in December 1987, the Ontario Human Rights Commission announced its decision—the Ontario Hockey Association had discriminated against Justine. They also said that Section 19(2) in the Ontario Human Rights Code was unconstitutional because of Section 15 in the Canadian Charter of Rights and Freedoms and that it must be taken out of the Code. Justine, and other girls who made boys' teams, had to be allowed to play.

It was a huge victory for people who believe in human rights. Right across Canada people celebrated because a twelve-year-old girl stood up to what she and the people who supported her saw as bullying. By now Justine was fifteen years old. Her brother, David, was playing for another team called the Toronto Eastenders in a new age category. This was the team she would have been playing on had she been allowed to continue to play.

When Justine won the court decision she thought, "This is amazing!" She phoned her new coach to let him know she could play, but his answer stopped her cold. He told her that she couldn't play because he had given her playing card away the night before to a player named John. Justine couldn't believe her ears. John hadn't even made the team. He had never even been on the team when there were tryouts. So why was he suddenly on the team now? Her new coach told her that they had just decided to do it, and the decision was final.

Justine hung up the phone, devastated. All that effort and hurt—for nothing! But before she knew it, her brother picked up the phone and called the coach back. He told the coach to give his spot to Justine and promptly quit the team. David knew that as a boy he could find a new team in a week, which is what he did. Justine's biggest supporter was her brother. He said, "If I can do it, you can do it too."

Justine went on to play for the women's Varsity Blues team at the University of Toronto a few years later. She only wanted to play with boys who were the same size, but once the boys became much taller and bigger, she knew she would go back to female hockey. She would be old enough by then to play against older women, who took their hockey seriously. She also played for the Toronto Aeros, one of the legendary teams in Canada because they have dominated women's hockey for so long. At this time Angela James and Justine Blainey were teammates. Justine won two national titles, and several provincial titles with the Aeros.

At university she studied science and then entered chiropractic college, where she learned how to treat people with sore backs and other mechanical disorders of the joints. Like many other athletes, Justine wanted to help people with injuries. By the time athletes have completed their competitive career, they usually have had plenty of injuries themselves. Now she is Dr. Blainey and, as a chiropractor, believes in treating the whole person. She's not interested just in a back injury, but in the person who has the sore back, and why they think their back is sore. Her journey from being the little girl who wanted to play with the boys to being a strong and confident woman was very rough and hurt an awful lot, but it also taught her to ask questions. Maybe a person is hurting on the outside because there is pain on the inside too.

Today, at twenty-nine years old, Justine plays against the Aeros (who are now the Beatrice Aeros) for the Brampton Thunder team in the National Women's Hockey League. She's had two children in the past few years, so she's had to take some time off the ice, but at least twice a month she talks to kids in school about why it is important to stand up for everyone's human rights. Much has changed since Justine bravely took on the hockey traditionalists. It is because of this hockey player's fight that so many girls and women have the freedom to play on the best team possible.

Lindsay Bach:
Dancing Through Life

When Lindsay Bach was a little girl and her family lived in Peterborough, Ontario, her mom loved every sport imaginable, and she encouraged Lindsay to participate in all of them. Lindsay took to sports immediately, but while she loved tearing around and playing games, her heart kept telling her to dance. Soon after she learned to walk, she taught herself all kinds of dances, making them up just the way other kids make up little songs. When she was five, Lindsay started ballet classes, and when she turned six, she also tried out tap and Highland dancing. Lindsay says there's a Scottish part to her that wants to find its roots while she dances in a kilt. She also loved gymnastics when she was young, but by the time she turned twelve or thirteen, her mother, Julie, told her she had to make a choice—gymnastics or dancing. By then Julie was raising Lindsay on her own, with help from Lindsay's grandparents, who were hoping she would follow her heart and choose to dance in the fashion she loved best.

But just as Lindsay was thinking that dance would win over gymnastics, she and her mom moved to Alberta. Lindsay would have to find a new teacher and dance school to join. She was starting grade nine, which is a big jump in someone's life, even if she hasn't moved two time zones to a new home and city.

COURTESY JULIE BACH

Lindsay took some classes at Alberta Ballet but didn't feel comfortable there. She realized she just didn't have a passion for ballet, and that she found the exactness of the dance too restrictive. In ballet, your arms and legs have to be perfectly positioned at all times. "You have to have your arm just this way," says Lindsay. "So I chose jazz and modern dance."

Lindsay likes the African origins of jazz dancing. "There's a kind of joy, it's not commercial. It feels like such true dancing. It's honest. In ballet you have to be so proper. Jazz, you are living the music. You feel it because it is very syncopated and rhythmic. I said to myself, 'Why not stay here and try to develop something . . . be one of the up-and-coming people?' "

Since Lindsay made the decision to concentrate on jazz and modern dance, she's tried to take as many classes and workshops as she can. When she was only in grade eleven, in the summer of 2001, she auditioned for the Bates Dance Festival, at Bates College in Lewiston, Maine. The festival is a big affair for dancers, and competition to perform there is stiff. She was the only Canadian to successfully make it through the audition, but then realized she couldn't possibly afford to attend the festival. For many kids like Lindsay, who come from single-parent families, the arts (and sports too) are just too expensive. Being a good dancer or athlete costs money now, and not everyone—even when they are really talented—has parents who can afford to pay their way. Lindsay would be responsible for her own travel and accommodation. Young dancers need to eat well too. The costs started adding up in her head.

Lindsay's mother suggested she apply to the Alberta Foundation for the Arts, which, at the last minute, came through with enough funding for her to attend. The experience in Maine, where she danced with young people from all over the United States, was one of the most wonderful

Lindsay ever had, and quite a contrast from some of the things that had happened to her at her first school in Calgary.

Lindsay was born with a birthmark on her face, and some kids teased her or were unfriendly. She has had many operations and laser treatments at the Boston Hospital burn unit, courtesy of the Shriners Club in Calgary, which pays for her visits. As she grew older, the birthmark faded, but she was still teased. When she and her mother moved to Calgary when Lindsay was going into grade nine, she says, she had looked forward to the move. "I was really confident in grade eight, I knew everyone, and so coming to Calgary made me really excited. I had high expectations, I was going to meet new people.

"I went to school and I was so nice to everyone. I was myself, that's all I've ever been, but they didn't want to accept me. I was so glad I was still dancing, because so many girls give it up when they turn twelve, but at fourteen I hated being here in Calgary so much, I just looked forward to dance. Everyone accepts me there."

Lindsay stood out during the first year, grade nine. Not only was she dancing, she made the school volleyball and cross-country running teams too. The next year she switched to another school in Calgary, which she liked much better. Still, it was dance, not school, that continued to be the focus of her life. "It's like a different language," she says of dance. "All dancers have this connection—you understand one another, it's almost like a secret club. Some people might think we are snobs, but we're just as insecure as everyone else. I mean, okay, I have a birthmark. I look different, but when I am dancing, I am no different from the other dancers. I don't notice myself. I just get lost in the dance."

The summer after she graduated from high school, Lindsay auditioned for a place in the University of Calgary's dance program. It's a tough program because it combines the fine art of dancing with many of the science classes of physical education. You have to have high marks, but you also have to dance your way into class. She was on pins and needles all summer, hoping she would be accepted for fall classes.

Meanwhile, she enrolled in an intensive week-long workshop at Decidedly Jazz dance studio in Calgary. This company has a reputation of producing very professional and exciting dance. The instructor, Jamie Freeman-Cormack, had them dress up as gangsters with big hats and suits for the final show. "She wanted the audience not to know," says Lindsay. "Who is male, who is female, who is good, who is bad? You get to act, be a different character. In dance you don't have to be yourself." Acting, she says, is very much a part of dance.

The Decidedly Jazz lessons were the last week of formal dancing Lindsay would be doing before she started her job at the downtown YWCA that summer. She would soon start work as a camp counsellor, and she wanted to get in as much dancing as she could before her responsibilities there started. Only twelve students would be accepted into the University of Calgary program, but Lindsay felt she'd danced well in the audition, and she wanted to be ready in September if she got accepted.

Lindsay knew she needed to prepare for her university dance classes in other ways. Dancers need plenty of strength and endurance, and they need to be able to focus intensely on what they are doing. Once work started, she would be able to use the Y's gym for free. "I like to use the weight room, and take full advantage of the membership," she says. On top of this, she bikes, in-line skates, and does yoga—which she loves. "You realize with yoga that your mind is always thinking. The truth is, sometimes you want to not think about anything." Lindsay says the most important aspect of yoga is breathing, and if you really meditate on this, your mind will clear.

One day when Lindsay came home from her job at the Y, she learned that she was one of the lucky twelve students accepted into the dance program at the University of Calgary. She was filled with joy when she received the letter of acceptance, but says she had felt good about her chances all along. "The first day of auditions at the university was to get us used to it there and relax. We did an orientation dance class with everybody in it, but after that, not everyone stayed," recalls Lindsay. "I was really nervous, but at the same time I knew I would get in because I had prepared well. But I didn't want to be overconfident. Sometimes I hold myself back. I don't want people to think I am a snob."

Dance is complicated, Lindsay says, and a dancer has to be prepared for criticism. "They're helping you when they criticize, but you tend to be a critic on yourself," she says. "It can be tough to hear so much criticism. After a while, all you want is a hug and for someone to say, 'That was good.' The best thing, though, is when you come out of the dressing room, all your role models—the dancers you watched when you grew up—are there in the same studio. Then you see that they're just people too."

In September 2002, Lindsay started her university classes. Who knew where dance would lead? Many dancers from the university became full-time professional dancers or instructors themselves. Lindsay and her mother celebrated her hard work that fall. "My mom, she tells other people how proud she is of me. She supports me no matter what. She's so proud."

Though it was hard for both of them, Lindsay decided in her first year that she wanted to live in residence on the university campus and apart from her mom, who is also one of her very best friends. She wanted to be as independent as possible. Being so close to school was great, and Lindsay flourished in the atmosphere, not only of a good dance program but of excitement in a big university. Still, despite how exciting everything seemed, there was plenty of work. To receive a Bachelor of Fine Arts degree in dance, she was expected to take science, phys. ed., and social science courses too. On top of this, she was in two dance productions. One was Alberta Dance Explosions, which was a three-week festival in February 2003 put on by Dancers' Studio West, another dance organization like Decidedly Jazz. Then in April, the students put on "Dance at Noon" at the university, so other students could see what their program was about.

"A lot of people from other faculties think the program is a joke because all we do is dance, but that isn't the case," says Lindsay. "I will tell you that it is not easy to get an A in a movement-based class. We also have to take options from a number of faculties including Kinesiology, Social Sciences, and the Humanities."

Lindsay enjoyed her studies and the performances, but at the end of the year, she decided to move back home. She could commute to school on Calgary's C-Train in the fall. "I think I've changed a lot since beginning school," she says. "I've definitely learned a lot more about the realities of life. One of the major issues is money! I would love to travel and take dance, but it is tough when you are trying to save money for school."

Lindsay did get to travel during the summer of 2003, once school was over. She was able to do a "travel study" to Guinea in West Africa for three weeks. The university course was offered by the dance faculty, and it was during this trip that Lindsay found the roots to her beloved jazz dancing. "This was absolutely life-changing," she says. "We danced and drummed and lived with the people. I've learned a lot about people and myself. My Africa trip taught me so much. It is difficult for me to even know how much I've changed because I've had so many new experiences."

COURTESY JULIE BACH

When Lindsay returned to classes in the fall, she had to get used to a student's life again. She had been lucky to have such wonderful experiences in Africa, but in her second year at school, she had to make room in her busy dance life for Human Anatomy classes. After all, if dancers are going to use their bodies, they should also understand how those bodies work. The class is "extremely challenging," says Lindsay. "We do labs with cadavers (dead bodies) regularly." Despite the tough classes, Lindsay is trying out for "Mainstage," which is the university's big dance production for the year. She will have to commit to three 2-hour rehearsals each week from December to the spring when the dance will be performed.

Being a full-time student and a dedicated dancer is pretty tough, but Lindsay wouldn't have it any other way. "To be completely honest, I just want to be a dancer," she says. "I have already taken a somewhat safe route by getting a university education, so there will be many options in my field. I look at my future in terms of goals that are achievable. Teaching dance in junior high or high school may be an option someday."

Lindsay believes it is important to be happy with her life and to be a healthy human being—and dancing, for her, accomplishes both. Her advice to girls is to make sure they take care of their bodies "and that means feeding it properly," she adds. "Go out and get inspired, see shows, have mentors, travel, keep a journal, don't worry about the future too much. Try to live in the moment and enjoy where you are right now."

Daria Gaiazova:
Gliding Her Way into a New Land

Ever since she was a little girl in Russia, Daria Gaiazova has liked to cross-country ski. "I always loved the forest," she says, "and I loved to race." Cross-country skiing is perfect for someone like Daria (who prefers to be called "Dasha," which is what her friends and family call her).

Dasha loves Nordic skiing because it offers the quiet of the woods in wintertime but can be very competitive and technical as well. When she lived in Russia, in no time at all, Dasha had joined the Babuschkemo Ski Club in her town of Poshcheno, 120 kilometres outside Moscow. But though she loved her club and was happy to ski in Russia, her parents were planning a big change in the family's life.

"My dad is a scientist and he said he always wanted to work abroad," says Dasha. "But there were two other reasons my mom and dad decided we should leave Russia," she adds. "They thought it would be good for us to live somewhere else, and they were afraid my brother would have to fight in

Chechnya if we stayed in Russia." She is referring to the ugly war between Russia and its southern neighbour.

And so the Gaiazova family started to research what country they should move to. Both of Daria's parents are microbiologists, and the family's town, Poshcheno, was a science village where many of Moscow's scientists live. "In Russia we have many science villages. Most of my friends there had scientists for parents, and now many of them live all over the world."

Dasha's parents decided to move to Toronto. Dasha was fifteen while her brother was about to turn thirteen. Like many immigrants, the Gaiazovas saw Toronto, with its extraordinary multicultural environment, as the best possible place to settle. But when they arrived, the city wasn't exactly what they had been hoping for. "In Toronto I tried to train for cross-country skiing," says Daria. "But I was by myself, had no coach, and I really missed my club—the Babuschkemo Ski Club. I thought my ski career was over."

Dasha's parents, as well, didn't really like Toronto that much and soon her father found a job in Montreal.

"I immediately loved Montreal," says Dasha. "I

was running on Parc Mont Royal, right in the city, and I saw a guy roller-skiing and asked him if he could give me the number of a coach." Roller skis are short skis on wheels similar to in-line skate wheels. They have bindings so skiers can wear their ski boots and train in the summer when they aren't cycling or running. Skiers use special poles with extremely hard carbide tips so they can dig a little into the pavement but don't break off.

CROSS COUNTRY CANADA

Dasha received the right phone number, but when she called it turned out that Luc Germain didn't speak a word of English or Russian, and at the time, Dasha didn't speak a word of French. "But we communicated and I joined the club Ski Elite."

Now she could compete in the sport that had stolen her heart and enjoy her new city. "My mom and I love the jazz festival every summer, we love the cafés and the street life. Everything about the city, I love." As it turned out, Dasha thrived at her new ski club as well. "My coach was really kind and got me roller skis (for summer training) and the right clothing. I think he saw my potential, and I went to my first Canadian nationals in 2001. In Russia I wasn't super-great, just the best skier in my club, but the competition there is fierce. You must be exceptional from the time you are a little kid, or you are forgotten."

At the Junior Canadian Championships Dasha competed in four races and came fourth in every one of them. But she also skied on the Quebec team that took the silver in the relay, and this medal became the first of many national medals she would win in Canada. People were wondering who this new girl was. At seventeen she appeared out of nowhere, and she was fast. She missed a bronze medal by half a second in one race. Dasha knew she could beat her new competition and decided she wanted to improve upon her placings. "Ever since then I don't want to finish fourth again," she says with a laugh.

Her solid finishes at the Junior Canadian Championships allowed Dasha to be invited to the Junior Development National Team in the 2001–02 season, and she kept improving at such a rate that she qualified for the team that would be sent to the Junior World Championships. But despite her speed she couldn't go.

"You have to be in Canada for three years before you can apply for Canadian citizenship," she explains, "and I still had eight months to go." Cross-Country Canada could have made a special arrangement for Dasha so she could compete for her new country, but they didn't. The paperwork just never got done. Instead of getting really down about it, Dasha became more determined—she studied French and English well, and boned up on her Canadian history for the citizenship test. In September 2002 she passed with flying colours, as did the rest of her family. "We went out for a celebration dinner," she says, "and then I had my passport and I knew I could compete at the World Championships and hopefully the Olympics someday for Canada."

Since her first national championships in 2001, Dasha has won plenty of medals. At the beginning of the 2002–03 season, when she was in her last year as a Junior woman and her first year as a student at Montreal's McGill University, she raced against senior American and Canadian women in the Continental Cup races in Western Canada. The Continental Cup pits North America's best against one another. In a total of six races, Dasha placed in the top three every time.

In early January, while she was still a Junior, she went to the tryouts for the Junior team, the Under 23 team, and the Senior team. She surprised everyone, but mainly herself, when she made all three teams!

"I was shocked," says Dasha. "I was preparing for the Canada Games, and now I have a chance to go to the Senior World Championships. But when I really started to look at the schedule, I realized I would have to go to Europe in January for the Junior Worlds, and then stay all the way through until early March in order to do all the competitions. I was in school at McGill and I wanted to finish my courses, and I just didn't know what to do."

Dasha asked others who had spent most of the season racing in Europe what they thought she should do, and they told her there would be plenty of time to go to the Senior Worlds later in her life. Dasha is one of the best cross-country skiers ever to come from Canada (even if we did import her), and she could race well into her thirties. In the end, Dasha decided not to rush her skiing career, and instead to make sure she was well prepared for her first Senior World Championships. She would go to the Junior World Championships in Sweden, where she placed sixteenth in the 5-kilometre classic ski event (classic skiing means the skier moves with a diagonal stride—left arm forward while the right leg is kicking, and then when they bring their body weight to the centre of the skis, they quickly change so their right arm is forward while their left leg is kicking). She had two other top-thirty performances there, and started to realize how tough it was going to be to crack the top ten in her sport. "When I went into the Junior Worlds," she says, "I was rated in the top ten in the world, but the point system they use is deceiving. People are away from some of the races leading up to the Worlds, or they start really skiing hard when they get to the Championships.

"It was an entirely new experience, and super fun. In the end I became really motivated because I was skiing with the best juniors in the world. You get there and these people are going so fast."

Dasha found out what many athletes discover when they go to their first World Championships or Olympics. The international rating can't be taken too seriously. Many people peak just for the World Championships and either don't go to very many of the events leading up to them, or train hard while they are racing in other events, which makes them tired for smaller races. But if they taper properly—which means they decrease the amount of training before the World Championships and get plenty of rest—often they can have their best races of the season.

Dasha returned from Sweden and had two major tasks ahead of her. She was in the Business faculty at McGill University as a part-time student, and she had missed plenty of classes; there was homework to catch up on. And then she had to go to New Brunswick and ski for the Quebec team at the Jeux Canada Games.

Skiing in Canada as a new Canadian and being covered for the first time by the Canadian media was a wonderful experience for Dasha. "I won two gold medals and two silver," she says, "and the media was fantastic. It gave me a chance to promote skiing, which I always want to do, and we showed how fast the skiers from Quebec can be. Unfortunately, Alberta beat us in the relay and we had to take the silver, but it was so close. I loved it."

Amid these wonderful athletic successes, Dasha believes in balancing her life. "As soon as I go back to Montreal after my races, I know there are exams," she says. "I race or train every day, but I study every day too. I take all my textbooks to the races, but I am only taking three courses instead of six, so I can go to Europe to race. I love the travelling that comes along with competition. I love being outside and in the forest with just my skis and skiing as hard as I can. I want to give my best every year."

She currently looks to the 2006 Winter Olympics in Italy as her biggest goal, and says the crackdown on drugs in her sport will help honest athletes. Some cross-country skiers have been caught taking performance-enhancing drugs at the Olympics and World Championships. Many people believe that a drug called erythropoietin, or EPO, that increases red blood cells is commonly used. Red blood cells carry oxygen to muscles, and if muscles get more oxygen they can work at a more efficient rate, especially if the athlete is using those muscles to run, ski, or cycle long distances. This is why some marathon runners, bike racers, and Nordic skiers are most likely to take this particular drug. In the past it has been difficult to test athletes to see if they are taking EPO, and many people believe there are plenty more who would test positive if the tests were more refined. The World Anti-Doping Agency (WADA) has been working on this, and someday these sports may be a little more fair. Dasha's teammate on the Canadian senior women's team, Beckie Scott, is leading the way. At the 2002 Salt Lake City Olympics, she challenged Richard Pound, the head of WADA, saying there were plenty of athletes on drugs. Mr. Pound replied that Beckie was wrong. But in just a few days, the two skiers who had come ahead of Beckie in her 5-kilometre pursuit event both tested positive in other events. Norway and Canada have done a great deal of work in anti-doping, and on October 21, 2003, a year and a half after Beckie should have received the gold, she was awarded the silver medal in her event, as one of the competitors was disqualified. In December, two months later, she was awarded the gold. The whole country celebrated. What brave and wonderful boots Dasha looks forward to filling!

Dasha hopes for the day when drugs aren't a problem in sport. Meanwhile, advises Dasha, don't lose the spirit of who you know you can be just because there are obstacles in the way.

"Hopefully it is better now in skiing, and better for fair play. WADA has put lots of pressure on athletes and their sports to be clean," says Dasha, who in just over three years has learned to speak English with eloquence. She arrived in Canada with only the bit of English she had learned in her classes at school. “No matter what your sport or your work is, you have to enjoy it. If you put your soul into what you do, you will be happy,” she says with a wide smile on her face and in her voice. “If you can’t find your soul and happiness, try something else.”

In February 2004, Dasha represented Canada at the U23 (ages twenty-three and under) World Nordic Ski Championships. She teamed up with Chandra Crawford from Canmore, Alberta, to win the bronze medal in the sprint relay. The course is 1.7 kilometres long, and the skiers complete it three times. The Italian team took the gold in 21:08 minutes, with the Swiss earning silver in 21:33 minutes. Just two seconds behind were the Canadians with their bronze medal–winning time of 21:35 minutes. Dasha had a big smile on her face as she accepted her medal. In just five years she had gone from thinking she might lose her favourite sport altogether, to standing on the podium at the World Championships with Canada’s maple leaf on her back. It’s been quite a journey for the girl from Poshcheno, Russia.

Faith McDonald:
Acts of Faith

"My grandparents, Nimosom and Nookom—that's what we called them in Cree—raised me to be a good kid," says hockey star Faith McDonald. "The day school was over my brothers and I would race to the shore of the lake because we knew they were taking us to their camp. We'd pitch a tent and then all summer we'd live under the stars, collect firewood, fish, hunt. It was a part of my life, so peaceful, quiet—a good time for you and your family. My grandparents were very experienced people. They knew everything about living on the land."

It is this family base, says Faith, particularly the guiding hands and hearts of her grandparents, her older brother, Desmond, and her friend and role model, Barb Moore, that took her through many trying times. Faith's grandparents taught her about love and tradition, her brother taught her love and hockey skills, and Barb taught her love and dedication. She drove Faith to games and tournaments in Northern

Manitoba's cold and wild winters, and took her canoeing in the summers. Barb provided an example of balancing sport with compassion for others that she would never forget. Faith has been a top forward on both the Manitoba and Alberta provincial hockey teams, and a role model in her own right. In the 2002–03 season, she enrolled at the University of Manitoba and soon became one of that province's best university players.

When Faith was little, there was no hockey arena in her community of Nelson House, which has a population of 2,000 people. She and her brothers, cousins, and friends played road hockey all winter and baseball in the summer. "I was the only girl, but that didn't matter to me or anyone else. I just wanted to play." Then in 1990, an indoor arena was built and kids were told to come down, sign up for Minor hockey, and not to worry if they didn't have skates or equipment. They could find them at the arena.

"I didn't want to go," Faith recalls. She was ten years old, and she thought being the only girl on a real team was different from being the only girl in a pickup road game. But she says her big brother, Desmond, practically dragged her down there, and they all signed up. She didn't have any skates or equipment, and her parents didn't have any money to buy them any, but most kids were in the same position. They managed to get outfitted with equipment that had been donated to the community, and started playing on ice.

It turned out that, at first, Faith wasn't the only girl. Others joined up, but only Faith stuck to the game, practising up to six hours a day, even on Christmas Day. "We'd eat breakfast, open our gifts, and then just play hockey all through the holidays. It kept us away from drugs and alcohol. I wouldn't have substituted anything for hockey, it's all I wanted to do."

Faith moved up in her age class from Atom to Pee-Wee, and Bantam, always as the only girl on the Nelson House Minor hockey team, but eventually she wondered what it would be like to play on a girls' team. The closest women's team was in Thompson, an hour away by car, and Faith was only in grade eight. Her parents didn't have a car, so she could only make it into town if she could find a ride. It was her friend Barb, her Uncle Ron, or her counsellor from the Band school, David Spence, who usually drove her there. She was recruited by Thompson's women's team, The Bad News Bears, when she was fifteen, along with her friend Michelle Monroe from Norway House, who was also the only girl on her community's team.

They went to the Manitoba Winter Games that year and won a bronze medal on the Northern Manitoba girls' team. Faith scored five out of nine goals in the final game. After an article about Faith appeared in the *Toronto Star*, the hockey coach at the legendary hockey high-school Notre Dame, in Wilcox, Saskatchewan, contacted the Nisichawayasihk Cree Nation. The school joined with the Band to offer Faith a hockey scholarship.

In grade nine Faith boarded with and played for Notre Dame. Then, in grade eleven, she was recruited by arch-rivals, the Lebret Eagles, a First Nations high-school team in Lebret, Saskatchewan, not far from Wilcox. She moved to Lebret that year and boarded and played with them during the school year. In the summer she stayed and played softball, her favourite warm-weather sport.

By 1997, she wasn't playing just for the Eagles, she had also made the Manitoba Midget team that played at the Canadian Championships, where they placed sixth. Faith was used to her team placing in the top three at tournaments and was a bit surprised by the top-notch competition at the Championships. It was a wake-up call to the player who had always been one of the best female stickhandlers in Manitoba and Saskatchewan. Now she was competing against girls from other provinces who were also top in their leagues. Scoring wasn't so easy, but Faith had a better idea of how hard she would have to train to be able to compete at the national level.

She still wanted to keep playing, but trying to balance hockey and school, and not having enough money to support herself, proved to be too difficult. She knew she needed to return frequently to Nelson House to try to help her family and community, but there wasn't the kind of hockey there that she needed to play. If she lived in the city, she didn't have enough money to play the game. Like many First Nations athletes in Canada, Faith didn't have parents or sponsors who could support her career. She would have to put her hockey dreams on hold. In 1998, she decided to go to school in Regina, and stayed with her baseball coach's family there, but found that ice-time for women barely existed. She would once again have to find rides to get to a women's team. She played for the Lebret team at All-Native Tournaments, but knew she wasn't being athletically challenged, and it was difficult to get rides to train with the team, which was a good 100 kilometres away.

Life then was often frustrating. All Faith wanted to do was play the best game of hockey she possibly could. But being First Nations and female in Canada didn't make that easy. Ever since Manitoba Hydro flooded the ancient hunting and fishing territories of the Nisichawayasihk Cree Nation in 1975, people had started to lose the traditions that had supported them for centuries. Faith's grandparents, Alex and Fanny Spence, had taught all the children how to live off the land, but the land and the creatures on it were being destroyed by hydro projects that sent power to the south and poisoned the northern environment. How could Faith's family support themselves after losing the livelihood of trapping, hunting, and fishing, passed down by their ancestors? A new pair of skates is impossible to afford when a family exists on welfare.

Added to this is the discrimination all girls and women face in sport. Ice-time was available for Faith if she played on a boys' team, but when she switched to a women's team in Regina, she found nearly all the ice in that city was given to boys' and men's teams. Women had to travel late at night to isolated rinks to play, even though everyone knew this was unsafe.

In 2000, Faith returned to Nelson House, feeling like she wasn't going anywhere. Her dream of being a hockey player seemed more and more difficult to achieve. Then a friend called and told her she was moving to Calgary—and did Faith want to come along and play in the Olympic Oval Women's Program?

The Olympic Oval Program is designed for female hockey players, and attracts the top players, not just in Canada, but often from other countries too. Hockey players train in the same area as speed-skaters, runners, soccer players, and cyclists. As hockey players play on the rinks inside the oval, speed-skating greats like Clara Hughes and Cindy Klassen skate on the oval around them. It's one of the top winter training sites in the world. But how could Faith afford the thousands of dollars it would cost to train and live in Calgary?

It turned out other people had read the article about Faith in the *Toronto Star* back in 1995. A woman named Mary Scott had become interested in Faith's hockey career, and she just happened to have started a trust fund for kids like Faith who had lots of talent and dreams,

GREG JOHNSON PHOTOGRAPHY

but not the money needed to act on those dreams. Mary wrote to Faith and arranged for Faith to get the funds and somewhere to live. The Nisichawayasihk Cree Nation helped her as well. Soon the hockey player from northern Manitoba was able to glide onto the ice with some of the best female players and coaches in the world.

In the 2000–01 season, Faith's team, the Oval Lightning, won the Senior AAA Women's Championships in Alberta with Faith playing centre. They placed fourth at the Canadian Championships, which was a little disappointing. Fourth is so close to third, and third is a bronze medal!

But Faith was happy to have gone to her first Senior Women's National Championships. When she returned to Calgary, though, and spring took over where winter had left off, she had another decision to make that in some ways was just as hard as playing at the Nationals.

Back in Nelson House, Faith was becoming a well-known role model. Kids looked up to her and wanted to know how to play as well as she did. She knew she could work all summer in the recreation department there. But the Olympic Oval Program also offered summer training camps. If she stayed in Calgary and trained hard all summer, there was a chance that she could move up the Canadian hockey ladder—and everyone knows how difficult that task is.

In the end, Faith chose to return to Nelson House and work for the recreation program. "I've learned so much," she says. "It's my job to pass that knowledge on to the next group of kids coming up." She also got to participate in the annual canoe races with Barb—who made her work hard in the competition. And in the end, their crew won.

While Faith was home for the summer in 2001, she received some exciting news from Winnipeg. She had won the Manitoba Youth Aboriginal

Achievement Award in the sport category! Three months later, on a chilly October evening, Faith and thirteen other young Aboriginal achievers were honoured by a crowd of 1,200 people. It was pretty tough for Faith not to cry as she gave her acceptance speech, and a couple of times, she even had to stop for a while and let a tear roll down her cheek. She found out she wasn't a hit just on the ice, she was pretty good in front of a microphone too.

Faith played one more year in Alberta for the Oval Extreme in the 2001–02 season, and then there was another decision to make. By now she was almost twenty-two years old. It was time to go on to post-secondary education. She was interested in psychology and sociology, and she also wanted to help more girls in Manitoba play hockey. She would go back to her home province, continue her education, and contribute to women and girls' sport there.

But soon after she made that decision, tragedy struck. In the spring of 2002, Faith's beloved older brother, Desmond, the one who had taught her so much about hockey and insisted that she was good enough to play with boys, died in a car accident. He was only twenty-four years old. Faith was devastated.

"Desmond was such a good big brother. He always waited for me and said I should be on his team," she recalls. "We played hockey and baseball together, so in the summer there was a ball tournament in his memory and the whole team signed the ball and gave it to my family." She adds, "Sometimes it's pretty hard."

In the fall of 2000, Faith had lost a cousin her age to suicide and now Desmond was gone too. But Faith had faith. That summer she was one of the coaches at the North American Indigenous Games when a number of young people from Nelson House made the Manitoba team in canoeing. Now she was at the shoreline, not jumping into her grandparents' boat or taking instructions from Barb, but setting up canoes for the kids on her team. Nimosom and Nookom and Barb had taught her well.

That fall she enrolled at the University of Manitoba and made their varsity hockey team. In the spring she was chosen for a Winnipeg area select senior women's team that toured Germany and Austria.

As she continues her studies, Faith isn't sure whether she will dedicate herself for several years to trying to make the national hockey team, or spend more time and energy where she knows it is so needed—in First Nations communities. She may try to do both. Right now, she says, what she most wants to tell Aboriginal young people is to "keep going. There's so much more out there than there is in this little world of yours. It's within yourself—if you really desire it. I exceeded the limits of what I expected myself to do, and so can you."

Melissa Matthews and Her Mom: A Bicycle Built for Two

Sometimes we think that great girl athletes are those who make it to the medal podium. But there are plenty of other kids around who try just as hard as any Olympic athlete—it's just that they have to put in that effort every single day in order to cope with their disabilities. We praise Olympic medallists—and they deserve our praise—but sometimes the most courageous and interesting people are right in our own neighbourhoods. Melissa Matthews and her mom are an example.

When Melissa was born in 1987, her mother, Colleen, thought her daughter's birth went just fine. On the second day she was at the Victoria, B.C., hospital, however, the orthopedic surgeon came to visit her and told her they would have to put casts on Melissa's legs. Colleen started to cry. She soon learned that Melissa had bilateral club feet. Doctors fixed her baby's Achilles (the tendon that attaches the heel to the calf). They hoped this would straighten out her feet. Eventually Colleen was able to bring Melissa home.

But three months later, when Colleen went into Melissa's room to check on her, she thought her baby was shivering; in fact, Melissa was having a seizure. Colleen rushed her daughter to the hospital, only to find out she had a major infection. Melissa spent the next two or three weeks in the hospital in intensive care. Then the doctors realized her urine was backing into her kidneys. In the months that followed Melissa didn't gain any weight, she didn't cry, she didn't suck. Melissa had a grand mal seizure and was rushed to Vancouver Children's Hospital on the mainland. Colleen knew something was drastically wrong.

The doctors there ran many genetic tests. Finally they told Colleen that her daughter had a small piece of her fourth chromosome missing. This is a rare condition called Wolf-Hirschhorn Syndrome, which makes the chromosome look like a "short arm." All of Melissa's other chromosomes were fine, but this small change on the fourth one would make a big difference to the lives of everyone in her family.

Melissa lives in Esquimalt, just outside Victoria, B.C. This is a beautiful part of Canada for cycling, as people ride bikes year round in its warm climate, along hundreds of kilometres of bicycle trails. For years Colleen tried to figure out a way she and Melissa could go cycling together, but somehow she just couldn't find a solution. She knew Melissa would love the feel of the wind in her face while wheeling down the Galloping Goose Regional Trail that snakes all over the city and well into the countryside. The problem was, Melissa could not ride a bike. Wolf-Hirschhorn Syndrome prevents her from having the coordination for cycling, as well as other characteristics you need for cycling, like knowing how to read stop signs and which way you have to turn. When the rest of the family went for a bike ride, Melissa and her mom stayed home.

COURTESY RUTH LAYNE

Still, when people rode by Melissa on their bicycles, she was delighted. Colleen knew a special trailer would have to be custom made and would be awfully expensive. The family already had many expenses in caring for Melissa. But she set out to find a solution.

Colleen had put the word out in her community about Melissa, asking if anyone knew how she and her daughter could cycle together. One day, in the spring of 2001, the phone rang at the Esquimalt Police Station where Colleen works. It was the Esquimalt Lions Club. They said they'd like to purchase a special trailer for Melissa. A man named Tony Hoar built bicycles and bicycle trailers and lived on the other side of Malahat Mountain, 40 kilometres away. He could make a custom-made trailer with a seat that would attach to Colleen's bike. In fact, he had designed the wheelchair Rick Hansen used for his Man in Motion tour when he wheeled around the world. Who could ask for more? Soon mother and daughter, age thirteen, were riding together. "Melissa can't talk, but when she sees her bike helmet coming out, she gets really excited," says Colleen today. "My other daughter, Rachel, loves cycling, so now we can all go as a family."

Even though the Matthews family was very

strong, and tried to find solutions to help make Melissa's life more comfortable, Colleen joined a support group for parents of children with disabilities. There were eight mothers, all of whom had children about the same age. "It's so nice to talk with other parents who face similar problems," says Colleen, "and sometimes they know way more than the experts at the hospital when it comes to what's best for their children.

"The doctors told me Melissa had to wear special orthotic shoes for her club feet, and we made her wear them until she was ten years old," says Colleen. "But she was so active, she was far more coordinated than they thought she was, and the shoes rubbed her feet. She had raw sores all the time. It was terrible. Finally we threw them in the garbage. Over the years since then she's strengthened her feet a great deal. Now she goes for long walks on the ocean, something the doctors never thought she could do. When we went to Spokane in the United States for a gathering of kids with Wolf-Hirschhorn Syndrome, only Melissa and one other girl could walk. We're so proud of her."

It's been a long and difficult journey for Melissa and her family to reach the point where Melissa has such wonderful mobility and freedom, but it's taught Colleen a lot about love. "Melissa was three when Rachel was born," says their mother. "By the time she was two, Rachel was being a little mother to Melissa. Then Melissa started mimicking her younger sister. Even before that, Rachel was helping her out. She started to walk at a very young age—at only ten months. Once Rachel started walking, Melissa started walking. It was the same thing with food. Rachel taught Melissa how to eat properly. Today Rachel and Melissa get ready together for cycling. My daughter has always had a special place in her heart for people with special needs."

These days when Melissa is so able to cope with a world that isn't set up very well for people with special needs, it's hard to imagine what it was like when she was just a baby. "When Melissa had her grand mal seizure and she stopped breathing as a baby, that could have been the end," says Colleen. "But we all worked hard. We joined the nursery with the other special needs children, and now the kids are fifteen years old. I couldn't have got through all of this without lots of support. But Melissa also gives me plenty of support. She has a great sense of humour—she likes slapstick—and she laughs at everything. She's crazy about action sports, especially anything with a ball. Her eyes don't go off the ball."

In 2002 Melissa was in grade seven. From kindergarten on, she and the other kids at the special needs nursery were integrated into mainstream classes. Each of them had a teaching assistant so they could learn at their own speed. But a new government took over in B.C. in that year and made huge cuts in education. They fired the teaching assistants, and Melissa and her friends fell way behind. "She would go to school and just sit there," says her mom. "It was terrible."

Finally the special needs children were put in a class of their own and are flourishing again. "Outside of school I teach Melissa all the life skills I can," says Colleen. "We go swimming twice a week and horseback riding once a week. She loves to come grocery shopping and put things in the buggy. When we want to bake cookies together we go to the store and she picks out the ingredients. Melissa is very proud when she can help me out that way."

Colleen says most special needs children are overlooked. "All the other kids at the nursery would love to have a trailer too," she says. "But each one must be custom made to fit each child, and this takes a lot of time. There is no program that helps kids like this. We were lucky that the Lions Club decided to help us, but many other children need help. Each trailer has to be designed differently depending on the child's disability. North Park Bikes, a store in our town purchased a couple of the trailers and is donating them to families. An organization called Recreation Integration is really involved. They have young people volunteering and taking children out for bike rides on the Galloping Goose bike trail. The same guys take Melissa out sailing. She absolutely loves it. When they make standards for equipment, everyone thinks all the equipment is the same. To meet the needs of these kids, all the equipment must be different. It's very frustrating. I know of one little boy who desperately wants a bike trailer like Melissa's but his family can't afford it."

Colleen and her family will continue to work so all children have access to simple things like bicycle trailers and rides in sailboats that will make really positive changes in their lives; meanwhile, they put their helmets on nearly every day and ride the Galloping Goose trail.

Molly Killingbeck:
Taking a Chance

"I always had fun playing sport," says Molly Killingbeck. "In junior high I played volleyball, basketball, softball, dodgeball, and did track and cross-country running. But it was just lots of fun. I remember watching the 1976 Olympics in Montreal when I was sixteen, and not in my wildest dreams did I think that I—Molly Killingbeck—could do that."

Molly *did* go to the Olympics. She won a silver medal as a member of the 4x400 relay team at the 1984 Los Angeles Games, and then coached the men's 4x100 relay at the 1996 Olympics in Atlanta when they won the gold medal. She has had a profound effect on this country. Not only has she represented Canada as a runner from 1980 to 1988, and coached many other athletes at the World Championships and Olympics, but she also takes plenty of time to visit kids in schools. Added to this is her long-time participation in and then support of the Harriet Tubman Games in Toronto each summer. These games bring together kids from all over Canada and parts of the United States and the Caribbean to run and learn about the history of African-Canadian people. Talking to kids in schools and getting them out to the Tubman track meet are what she now loves best.

"Part of my message to kids is that I am no superstar," she says, "but I gave myself a chance and so should they—just to see what happens."

Molly was thirteen when she came to Canada from Jamaica, and she says she was the shyest person on earth. She didn't know a soul in this country called Canada, and everything around her—the snow, and ice, the huge size of the country, and the bustle of Toronto—was new. Everything, that is, except for sports. She had loved sports in Jamaica and she carried that love north. And of all the sports she enjoyed, she was most devoted to running.

From grade ten on, she was fast enough to qualify for the Ontario high-school championships, known as OFSAA, but she never won a medal there. "My best finish was fifth. I was just so excited to go, and had so much fun seeing all these different cities in Ontario, I wasn't so concerned about winning. It was a chance to get out of the city and travel."

Still, she joined a track club outside of high

school and travelled from Toronto's east end, where she lived, to train at a track in the west end. Her club's name was RAP (Reunited African People), and the talent in that club made Canada's track team stand out internationally. Canada has never again had so many young people come out of the Greater Toronto Area who competed on high-school teams and joined RAP or other grassroots clubs and then made it onto the national team. Back in the 1970s, training facilities were, for the most part, free to use, and clubs pitched in to make sure all talented athletes had a chance. It was the time of Angela Bailey, Angela Taylor, Charmaine Crooks, Marita Payne, Desai Williams, Mike Dwyer, Tony Sharpe, Mark McKoy, Lyndon Fong, Milt Ottey, and the Hinds brothers—and soon even more high-school students who would represent their country. This was truly a legendary period in Canadian track and field, and almost all of these great athletes had come to Canada as children from the Caribbean.

Today lots of kids can't afford to participate in sports because of the expense. Many come from families that have little or no money. It's important to remember that if these kids don't make teams it's not because they aren't talented or don't have the desire, but because they can't afford to participate.

CARL ANDERSON

Molly was so glad she was able to join RAP. Not only were people fast, but they had a lot of fun running, playing jokes on one another, and just enjoying each other's company when they trained and travelled to meets together. In the winter they trained at what was known as the Pig Palace or Cow Palace, a rickety wooden track in the Agricultural Building at the Canadian National Exhibition grounds.

"We went upstairs to the track," says Molly. "It was wild—only 160 metres, so you had to be careful on the banking. No one ever wanted to fall because you'd have splinters in your bum for the next year." When they couldn't train there, on cold days the kids would run inside their schools. "We ran the halls," recalls Molly. "We never thought about things like shin splints and other injuries. We just ran. There was nothing sophisticated about what we did."

Molly says athletes were lucky then. Sport was

a big deal in school and everyone took phys. ed., usually until they finished high school. Running was a year-round activity for Molly and her friends. In the fall they would start the cross-country season, followed by the indoor track season in the winter. In spring they'd go outside again for the outdoor track season. Members of track clubs like RAP ran in the summer and the whole thing started again in the fall. "We joined the track club the way you would join a drama club or a library club. It just seemed like a fun thing to do. I didn't take it very seriously."

Despite all the fun she was having, Molly worked hard, and if she didn't take herself too seriously, other people did. She was given opportunities to compete against members of the national team, and she eventually realized she could be one of them. "I remember at the end of high school some of the kids I was competing against in track and field made the Canadian team to a meet somewhere. I said to myself, 'Hey, if they can do it, why can't I?' They weren't so much better than anyone else. But I didn't know how to set goals or that I could dream about such things. I had to teach myself to do that."

She made her first national team in 1980, and in 1982, she, Angela Issajenko (who had been Taylor before her marriage), Charmaine Crooks, and Jillian Richardson won the 4x400 relay race at the Pacific Conference Games in Australia. “I remember thinking, ‘Something could happen here,’ ” says Molly. “We were pretty fast, but the Australians assumed they were going to win. We beat them by an eyelash. They were shocked. I think these were my first meaningful Games. Before that I thought it was fun to travel and meet people, but now I finally realized we could win too.”

The next year they placed fourth in the 4x400 relay at the World Championships in Helsinki, Finland. “Everyone was there,” Molly recalls. “There weren’t any boycotts or people injured.” At the 1984 Olympics in Los Angeles, the team won a silver medal. But the Soviet Bloc countries had boycotted these Games and the athletes never did know how they would have fared had all the national teams been there. Still, they were getting faster and faster. If they trained for four more years, perhaps they could win a medal in Seoul, South Korea, when all the Olympians would be together again. The year before Seoul, they were fourth once again at the World Championships.

Everything looked great. The team ran fast enough to qualify for the final 4x400 relay. The relay events are the last competitions at the

Olympics. They are amongst the most prestigious too, with hundreds of millions of people watching from around the globe as countries vie to see who has the fastest team.

Then disaster struck. "I dropped the baton," says Molly of her final event at the 1988 Seoul Olympics. "I thought the world had ended. I cried until there wasn't any water left in the world for my tears." The team was devastated as they comforted Molly. They had looked forward to and trained for this day for four years. "It took me a long time to realize that at the end of the day I had dropped a piece of metal. In the big picture, it didn't matter to anyone else beyond my own little world. People were dying, not getting enough to eat, not getting clean drinking water. You have to put these things in perspective."

Molly retired from competition after the Seoul Games, but not from her sport. She'd earned an honours sociology degree from York University and was a teaching assistant for the North York Board of Education. But she was taking coaching courses too. Canada has a series of courses called the National Coaching Certification Program. Molly soon became certified at Level II, which meant she could coach provincial-level athletes. Out of the blue one day she received a call from the University of Windsor. They were wondering if she would like to be the sprint coach for the track team. "I never planned on going into coaching," says Molly, "but the North York Board was very good about letting me go, and I was in Windsor in no time."

Soon Molly enrolled in more coaching courses and received her Level III, so she could coach national team athletes. Today she has parts of her Level IV, which allows her to coach at the international level. Few people in Canada have completed this level. She says, though, that what's important in coaching can't always be measured in certificates. "The athletes I worked with knew I'd been there before. They trusted me. Coaches need to have lots of patience. There are no carbon copies in human beings," Molly adds. "Everyone is an individual with individual needs and the coach's job is to find out how she can best serve those needs." A good coach will create an environment where athletes reach their personal best. For some a personal best may eventually be a medal at the Canadian or World Championships. For others, it may mean finishing a race that they never thought they could finish.

The University of Windsor also had an interesting way of running their club. Anyone could join. You didn't have to be a track star who had graduated from high school with a fistful of medals. But you did need to come to practice and try your hardest. "We had no restrictions on who could come out," recalls Molly. "One girl had never run before in competition. But she came out. That girl made it to the nationals."

Another time the mother of one of Molly's athletes told her, "You made a difference in Dustin's life. The discipline he learned on the track transferred to his school work."

Molly spent six years coaching in Windsor and then was recruited by York University's track team. York is the home of the Metro Track and Field Centre, and has facilities that Molly and her teammates from the 1970s could only have dreamed about. Soon the York team was flying in national meets. Molly used to like to tease the girls on the team by saying she was going to enter their race too. Though she hadn't competed since 1988, she had kept in good shape and made her athletes think twice about slacking off. Who wanted a coach who was nearly forty years old passing them halfway through a sprint?

She only joked with the athletes about taking them on in races, but she was serious about other things. When York University hosted a meet at around Christmas, runners had to bring donations to the food bank as entry fees. Athletes sometimes lead charmed lives, and Molly didn't want any of them forgetting about other less fortunate people in the world.

While she was a university coach, Molly started to coach at the international level too. As a sprint specialist, she was one of the coaches who accompanied the Canadian track and field team to the Atlanta Olympics in 1996. At the time there was a bit of a grudge match between the Canadian men's 4x100 team and their American counterparts. It didn't cross the minds of the Americans that anyone else could win the men's 100-metre event—and then out of nowhere Canadian Donovan Bailey took it in 9.84 seconds, which was a world record.

"How could that happen?" they asked, even though Donovan went into the Games as one of the fastest men in the world. Now they wanted revenge for Donovan's win and they believed it would come in the relay. The Canadian team barely made it into the finals after they nearly dropped the baton in their heat. Molly was helping Andy McInnis, who was the head coach of the team, with the relay runners. "These guys need a woman's touch," she said after the heat. She took them to a quiet track far away from the Olympic stadium in North Carolina to practise until they had the baton exchange down pat. Sometimes the men's sprint events involve large egos. Molly was trying to remind the Canadian team not to waste their energy on seeing whether they or the Americans had the bigger egos, but to use it to simply run fast and well. Sometimes they needed a woman—especially one with Molly's international credentials—to bring them back to Earth.

"Andy was in charge of the big picture, the whole team," says Molly, "but I wanted the relay team to see the smaller picture. What we needed to do was not to think too much about it. Everyone was ready. Everyone could do what they do naturally, which is to run fast. All they had to do was take this little piece of metal and run around the track faster than anyone else."

There was something truly magical in the air when the Canadian team stepped onto the track for the final the next evening. It was a hot but calm Atlanta night. The mainly American crowd was going wild, believing their team was going to be triumphant. The four Canadians just set about their business. Foot stops had to be adjusted properly, dry runs had to be carried out smoothly, thoughts had to be collected.

Bruny Surin from Montreal was first up. He flew out of the blocks and ran like the wind until he made a perfect hand-off to Glenroy Gilbert. He kept the pace and did the same as Bruny—passing perfectly to Robert Esmie. Robert, whose nickname was Blast-off, blasted along the track to Donovan Bailey, who flew to the finish line ahead of the Americans and everyone else. Molly's team had won. In modern Olympic history only the German and Soviet teams had ever beaten the U.S. 4x100 team. Now Canada could be added to that list.

This was truly a moment worth remembering in Canadian history, but Molly believes it's no more important than getting a girl to go from never running to qualifying for the nationals, or getting a boy to expect more of himself in school because he does so well in track, or making sure runners contribute to a school's food bank.

In 1999, when Molly became pregnant, she decided once she became a mother, she would spend more time at home. The life of a full-time coach is spent mainly on the road and in other cities, as track athletes have an indoor and outdoor season. While she loved the four years of university life at York, it was time to get a job that would allow her to spend more time with her family. She became the Athletes Services Manager for the National Training Centre in Toronto, and is sometimes a coach for the national team when they go away to meets. One of the things she likes best, though, is to encourage kids—especially her four-year-old son—to just play and enjoy moving their bodies.

"I watch my friends doing crazy things like driving their kids all over the place for hockey. I pray I don't ever become one of them. For kids, the most important thing is that they enjoy sport. My son keeps asking me, 'Mom, chase me. Chase me!' So we have this game. It's really simple. Kids love simplicity. When I introduce them to running, I like to say, 'Let's take off our shoes. Let's feel the grass on the bottom of our feet.'"

It may seem that feeling the grass on your feet is a long way from a silver medal at the Olympics, but Molly believes they are related. If she hadn't loved the simple action of running naturally—through the grass or on a sandy beach—she wouldn't have been able to do all the hard work it took to win an Olympic medal in 1984. One of her jobs is to make sure athletes put sport into perspective.

"I want people to know there is life after sport. This is part of a journey we are all on and sport is only one stop. Now I love going for my half-hour runs in the morning because they balance me, but they're not about competition. At some point you have to reflect on your experiences and ask yourself, how do you make yourself whole? I'm not anyone special, and I never was. I just took a chance."

Kara Lang:
Record-Breaking Goals

After being on the road for most of the last two years, sixteen-year-old Kara Lang came home at midnight, on October 20, 2003. She met her mom, Moya, and dad, Brian, at Toronto's airport, and finally that night, she slept in her own bed. The Canadian women's senior national team had done better than anyone had expected—placing fourth in a stellar run at the World Cup of soccer in the United States. The next morning Kara went back to her classes at St. Thomas Aquinas High School in Oakville, Ontario, where she is an honours student.

Kara is following her heart in the game of soccer, but she says it's because of her family that she is able to do that. "My family plays a huge role in my life," she says, after her first day back at school. "I wouldn't be doing what I'm doing if it wasn't for them. I am able to live on my own because of the way they brought me up. That's the only reason I can live halfway across the country." And, she may have added, miss three-quarters of her classes. Since February 2003, Kara has played not only for the Canadian team, but also for the Vancouver Whitecaps, three time zones away from her family.

Kara was born in Calgary, Alberta, in 1986, and shortly after that her family moved to Oakville, where she played in her local soccer league. She shone, and like other members of the national team when they were young, she started competing against older players. At tournaments her strong plays were noticed by reps from the Ontario Soccer Association (OSA), and soon she was invited to provincial training camps. She was also invited to train at the OSA's centre in Vaughan, north of Toronto, and made the trip from Oakville, which is west of the city, three times a week.

But Kara had another love and that was the sport of basketball, in which she played as a three guard (an essential position for sinking three-point baskets from outside the key). She competed on her school team and then joined the Burlington Panthers. Soon coaches from U.S. schools were scouting her and sending letters asking her if she would like a sports scholarship to their university when she graduated. The first letter from a U.S. university came while Kara was still in grade eight!

After grade ten, Kara had to face the fact that she had to choose her favourite sport. She had graduated from provincial training camps to national ones in soccer, and at fourteen, in 2000, she was named to the Under 19 National Team. "I saw a difference in opportunities," she says of the two sports. "I thought I could go further in soccer. Women's soccer was progressing and getting better every year." She no longer plays for the basketball team at her school, but still loves the game.

Kara also holds the distinction of being the youngest female soccer player in the world to score a goal in a senior international match. In November 2002 when Kara was fifteen years and 132 days old, she scored against Wales at the Algarve Cup. Up to that date, the great American player Mia Hamm (who was fifteen years and 140 days old) had held the record—quite the footsteps to follow, but if anyone could do it, it was Kara Lang.

In grade eleven in 2002, when she was still fifteen, Kara was named to both the Under 19 (U19) and the national senior women's teams. The combination made for a packed schedule with endless planes to catch to competitions all over the world and practices and games to attend. All the hard work led to the playing fields of Edmonton's

Commonwealth Stadium in August of that year, when Canada hosted the first ever Under 19 women's World Cup. In total during the 2002 season when she played U19, she had eight goals in sixteen games. Three of them came in the six games she played at the U19 World Cup.

DALE MACMILLAN / CSA

Twenty-five thousand people watched in the stands when the Canadian team played Denmark during their first game, and their fan base just kept getting bigger. The past Canadian record for fans out to a women's soccer game was 10,000 for the 1999 senior women's World Cup. Sportsnet broadcast the 2002 U19 World Cup games on TV, and registered 77,000 viewers for the Denmark game and then 108,000 when Canada played Japan. By the final game, Sportsnet registered nearly one million TV fans, which was far higher than its record set when they broadcast a Stanley Cup final the same year. Meanwhile more and more fans were coming to the actual games to cheer on the Canadian team. For the final, against the U.S., an astounding 47,784 enthusiastic fans packed the stadium.

In that final game, the two teams had to go into overtime as the score was still 0–0 by the end of regular time. For more than 100 minutes the two teams had played fast and hard. And then, finally in overtime, the Americans scored. The Canadian team felt as if they'd had their hearts kicked out. Kara especially was disappointed. If only she had had one of those magic goals that came earlier in the tournament. Then team captain Christine Sinclair took Kara aside and put the magic that had happened in those two weeks in Edmonton in perspective. She told her there were 50,000 fans screaming for them. Even when they lost, Canadians supported them completely.

It took a while, but Kara finally realized what they had done. "When we started this journey we never dreamed we'd be playing in the final on September 1 in front of 50,000 people," she said later. "We'll never forget this."

Great change was coming and the U19 team had a lot to do with that change. In the 2001–02 season, the Canadian Soccer Association had 307,258 registered female players. That figure increased to 342,976 in 2003, which was an 11.6 percent increase in one year. The team was inspiring women and girls across the country to take up this great game. Meanwhile, Kara had to get back to high school in Oakville. On top of attending classes, she was still going to play on the senior women's team at the Gold Cup in November of that year. A good placing at the Gold Cup, which includes North America, South America, and the Caribbean, would qualify the Canadian senior women's team to play in the 2003 World Cup.

Kara had already made her international debut on the women's senior World Cup team on March 1, 2002, when the team played against Scotland at the 9th Algarve Cup. During this tournament she scored four goals. Later, in July of that year, she played against Norway, the Olympic gold medallist team, at the France International Tournament. The Gold Cup, which was hosted by British Columbia, would be the next senior tournament she played in.

And boy, did she play! Kara was on the field for all five games. In one game alone against Jamaica, she scored four goals. By the end of this tournament, where the Canadians were once again beaten by the Americans in the final, the team had qualified for the World Cup in the fall of 2003.

Kara spent the winter training indoors and running in Ontario, and then on February 23, 2003, she signed with the Vancouver Whitecaps women's team and started her semi-pro career in the United Soccer League (USL). The USL is a North America–wide league with teams of men, women, and youth. The women's league within the USL is called the "W League." They play in the regional Pacific Coast Soccer League, which is a member of the USL. Kara packed her bags and moved to New Westminster, just outside Vancouver. She was the youngest player ever to be invited to play in the senior women's division.

By the time Kara had decided to play for the Whitecaps, she was sixteen, and would have to balance finishing grade eleven with meeting the team's competition schedule. She also had to attend national team training camps. Like most athletes who go to school, she packed her textbooks right beside her soccer cleats and sent her assignments in by e-mail. Her life may look glamorous on the outside because she flies around the world playing her favourite sport, but most of the time she spends just trying to stay on top of things, whether that's getting homework in on time or doing the drills the coach assigns.

When the Whitecaps signed Kara to their team they said, "Kara Lang is one of the most exciting young players in soccer today. She's the sort of player who can make things happen, with her skill, strength, and powerful shooting ability. And she is definitely a fan favourite."

People on the West Coast are mad about soccer, so Kara couldn't be in a better place. Often there is no snow all winter, and soccer-crazed people play year round. The Whitecaps play out of Swangard Stadium in Burnaby, on the outskirts of Vancouver. It seats 6,100 fans and has a great view of the mountains. Now it also has a great view of one of the best young soccer players in the world. In her first game, Kara scored two of the goals against the Okanagan Predators. The Whitecaps won 10–zip.

Still, Kara couldn't let the soccer-crazy environment take her away from her responsibilities as a student. She loves history. For her, learning history is like being told a story, and who doesn't like a good story? "I like the period between the two wars," she says. "So many interesting things happened that changed the world. I can't take as many courses as I'd like to," she adds, "because of my soccer schedule." But if Kara does take a course, she tries just as hard as she does on the field to understand what she is learning.

Playing women's semi-professional soccer was a great way for Kara to prepare for her first senior World Cup. When the Canadian national team regrouped near the end of the summer, Kara was ready for the world event. The coach of the women's team, Even Pellerud, knew he had brought a young team to play at this level—only the Brazilian team was younger—but he was confident in their abilities.

When Canada last entered World Cup competition in 1999, the results were terrible. The team lost every game. Not only were they out of that competition, but because of their poor showing, they also did not qualify for the Sydney Olympics. Veteran player Charmaine Hooper, who was also voted onto the World All-Star team, declared she would never again play for Canada's national team. She boldly called for the resignation of the team coach and went back to her club team in Chicago, saying Canada had loads of talent in women's soccer players but didn't have the equivalent talent in its coaches.

At first the Canadian Soccer Association denied the criticism Charmaine directed at them. But eventually they hired Even Pellerud, who had coached the Norwegian women's team to victory at the first women's World Cup in 1995. In the four years between the two World Cups, Canada's women's soccer program had built a stronger team. Charmaine was so impressed that she decided to come back and play for Canada in 2002. At age thirty-five she is still one of the top players in the world.

"Charmaine and our captain, Andrea Neal, are total mentors," says Kara of the two veteran players. "They're just so ready to give you advice, help you out. They're totally awesome."

But Charmaine was getting some really good help on the field in World Cup competitions from Kara too, who is half her age. Kara was developing the skills necessary for the team's international success. "I think with Kara Lang, she's an unusual specimen," Charmaine told the CBC during the World Cup. "She's been a great addition to the team with her strength and physical fitness. I think we'll see great things from her in our next games."

At the 2002 World Cup, Kara and her teammates played way beyond what people had imagined for the team, but it didn't happen immediately. In their first game against Germany, ranked third behind the United States and Norway going into the World Cup, they lost 4–1 and never seemed to really get into the game. They simply weren't as convincing on the field as they knew they could be. Next up was Argentina. The Canadians won this game 3–0, but they believed (and many watching believed) they didn't have it together in this match either. They were lucky Argentina had barely begun its women's program and had therefore sent an inexperienced team.

The final game in the preliminary part of the tournament was against Japan. It was do or die. Canada had to win this game to go into the quarter-finals. If they tied, Japan would move on, as they had scored more goals in international play since the last World Cup in 1999 than Canada had. (It had been decided before the World Cup had even started that tallying up past goals would be the first way in which tied teams would be selected for the quarter-finals.) Canada simply had to win. And from the very beginning, as they ran into the stadium in Foxboro, Massachusetts, on Saturday, September 27, Canada controlled the game. They decisively beat Japan 3–1. History had been made. There wasn't a team—male or female—in the history of Canadian soccer that had made it into the quarter-finals at the World Cup.

On Thursday, October 2, 2003, at 8 p.m. Pacific Coast time, Canada faced China, one of the top women's teams in the world and silver medallists in the 1999 World Cup. This time, the opposing team controlled the ball, and the Canadians didn't always look like they could hold on for the entire game. But two players shone—central defender Charmaine Hooper and goalkeeper Taryn Swiatek. At 7 minutes into the game, Charmaine scored, and even though the Chinese had plenty of shots on goal, Taryn kept all of them out. When the game was over, Canada had won 1–0, setting the bar even higher, as now they faced Sweden, another top international team in the semi-final.

Three days later on Sunday, October 5, in Portland, Oregon, the two northern teams faced one another. This time it was Kara's turn to shine as she scored Canada's only goal in the 65th minute of the game. But it just wasn't enough that night; Sweden scored two goals and won 2–1. The Canadians would be playing for the bronze medal, and it would be against their nemesis, the United States. "We've played them a lot and we know a lot about them—we can better prepare for them than any other team," said Kara as the team travelled to Los Angeles for the showdown.

Kara knew only too well how well matched the Canadians and the Americans were. In Edmonton the year before at the U19 final, she had played into overtime before the Americans won on a shootout. Three months later at the Gold Cup in Vancouver against the senior team, again they played into overtime, with the United States once more victorious. The Americans, like the Canadians, had some U19 players who played up to senior level.

On Saturday, October 11, they met the American team on American soil. It was an understatement to say that the home team was the favourite in the packed stadium. In the end, the Americans took the game 3–1—but the Canadians had arrived. They had taken the game to a place no soccer team in the history of the country had come close to before. They had started the World Cup as the twelfth best team in the world. Now, because of their spectacular performance, the team had finished fourth. All of Canada was very proud of their effort, but, just as she had after the U19 loss, Kara had mixed feelings.

"You hear 'congratulations' a lot. It took me a while to accept that, because I didn't think there was anything to be congratulated about. Fourth place is disappointing. I have to remember that we went farther than any Canadian team ever has in the sport."

In March 2004, Kara and her senior teammates had to accept an even larger setback in their quest to be the best they could be when they failed to qualify in the CONCACAF (North America, Central America, and the Caribbean) play-offs for an Olympic berth. Mexico, a team they had soundly beaten every time they had played them, won the game 2–1. The Canadian team didn't really play well together until the last fifteen minutes. By then it was too late. Canadian newspapers the next morning showed a devastated team.

No matter how shattered Kara felt about not going to the Olympics, she had to pick herself up and get ready for another qualifier in May, as the U19 team once again prepared for the U19 World Cup. At eighteen years of age, Kara was still a U19 player and would be on the field in Ottawa and Montreal against her CONCACAF rivals. If they placed in the top two there, they would go on to the U19 World Cup in Thailand in November.

As soccer makes its way internationally, things are changing at the club level too. In Oakville, where Kara developed her game, 9,700 players were registered with the Canadian Soccer Association for the 2003 season. Nearly 5,000, or 51 percent of those players, were female. If you compare those numbers to figures from 1981, when soccer was just beginning to be a big sport in Canada, the Oakville Soccer Club had only 3,600 players, and 500, or 14 percent, were females. Truly Canadian women and girls are causing a revolution in the game, and making history on the international playing fields. Kara—and her teammates—have plenty to be proud of.

Quizzes

SOCCER

Let's see how you dribble your way through this quiz.

1. How many players of any one team are on the field at a time?

   A. Eight
   B. Ten
   C. Eleven

2. Who is the only person who can catch the ball?

   A. A defenceperson
   B. A goaltender
   C. The coach

3. If you play forward you are:

   A. Offence
   B. Defence
   C. A goalie

4. You kick the ball with:

   A. The side of your foot
   B. Your laces (top of the foot)
   C. Both of the above

5. A chip is:

   A. When you kick the ball up and over in the air, with the inside of your toes
   B. When you throw the ball
   C. When you hit the ball with your knee

6. When throwing in from the sidelines, you must remember:

   A. To keep your feet on the ground
   B. To start with your hands behind your head
   C. Both of the above

Canoeing

Paddle through this quiz, and have fun. The canoe is a big part of Canadian history.

1. What Canadian city is famous historically as a meeting place for canoeists?

   A. Winnipeg
   B. Barrie
   C. Regina

2. What is the famous intersection in the city above?

   A. Bay and Bloor
   B. Portage and Main
   C. Sherbrooke and St. Laurent

3. If you are sitting in the back of the canoe, you are:

   A. The bowperson
   B. The passenger
   C. The sternperson

4. If you find yourself in a cedar dugout canoe, where are you most likely to be?

   A. The West Coast
   B. The inland lakes of Northern Ontario
   C. The coast of Baffin Island

5. If you are a recreational canoeist, chances are your boat will have:

   A. A relatively flat and stable bottom
   B. A sleek and aerodynamic profile
   C. A mast and sail

6. A recreational canoe usually sits:

   A. Two to four paddlers
   B. Five to eight paddlers
   C. However many there are paddles for

Track and Field

Jog, sprint, or jump through this little relay race.

1. What year were women first allowed to run the marathon at the Olympics?

   A. 1972
   B. 1984
   C. 1896—the same time men started running it

2. What is the sequence in the triple jump?

    A. A one-foot jump followed by a two-foot jump and then a step
    B. The standing broad jump, the high jump, and the triple jump done separately and then scores are added together
    C. Hop, step, and jump

3. What is the shortest distance for which you don't use starting blocks?

    A. 400 metres
    B. 1,500 metres
    C. 800 metres

4. What year did the Canadian women's 4x100 team win the Olympic relay?

    A. 1968
    B. 1928
    C. 1984

5. What did Debbie Brill invent?

    A. A type of running shoe
    B. An energy drink
    C. A revolutionary way of high jumping

6. Who was called the Saskatoon Lily at the 1928 Olympics?

    A. Bobbie Rosenfeld
    B. Ethel Catherwood
    C. Myrtle Cook

Hockey

Skate smoothly across the blue line on this one.

1. A tactic used frequently when a team is behind, near the end of the game is to:

   A. Injure the best player on the opposing team
   B. Remove the goalie and add another player to the line
   C. Complain to the ref that an opposing player should be in the penalty box

2. What Canadian player has played in every World Championship and Olympic Game up to 2002?

   A. Hayley Wickenheiser
   B. Cassie Campbell
   C. Geraldine Heaney

3. If you are offside you are:

   A. Across the farthest blue line before the puck
   B. Leaving the penalty box too early
   C. Having too many players on the ice

4. Each year the Canadian champions win:

   A. The Lady Byng trophy
   B. The Abby Hoffman Cup
   C. The Maureen McTeer Cup

5. The first full-time head coach for the women's national team was:

   A. Melody Davidson
   B. Danielle Sauvageau
   C. Shannon Miller

6. What female goalie played in the NHL?

   A. Sami Jo Small
   B. Manon Rheaume
   C. Angela James

Basketball

Don't pass the ball and miss the quiz!

1. The Canadian basketball team that has won the most games in the history of the nation is:

   A. The Toronto Raptors
   B. The Vancouver Grizzlies
   C. The Edmonton Grads

2. In 1976, when women's basketball premiered at the Montreal Olympics, who captained the Canadian women's team?

   A. Kendra Ohama
   B. Sylvia Sweeney
   C. Bev Smith

3. How much is a foul shot worth?

   A. One point
   B. Two points
   C. Depends on the foul

4. Running with the ball while you hold it is called:

   A. Double dribble
   B. Handling the ball
   C. Travelling

5. What team brought the Underwood Trophy back to Eastern Canada after the Second World War?

A. The Montgomery Maids
B. The Lakeside Ladies
C. The Humberside Honeys

6. What is the proper name used to describe the person you guard?

A. Your twin
B. Your check
C. Your mate

Cycling

Don't forget to breeze through this last bit.

1. The piece of metal that attaches the pedal to the bike is called:

A. The drive train
B. The pedal arm
C. The crank arm

2. Cycling first became an Olympic sport for women in:

A. 1968
B. 1984
C. 1896—the same time it became a sport for men

3. What Canadian has won four World Championships in mountain biking?

A. Clara Hughes
B. Sue Palmer
C. Alison Sydor

4. The distance between the bike saddle and the handlebars should allow elbows to be:

   A. Slightly bent
   B. Nice and straight
   C. Bent at a 45-degree angle

5. When descending in mountain biking, it's important to:

   A. Squeeze hard on the brakes whenever necessary
   B. Sit back in the saddle and use brakes when necessary, putting less pressure on the front brake
   C. Use the back brake to skid, especially on steep corners

6. Only one Canadian has won medals at the Summer and Winter Olympics. Her name is:

   A. Clara Hughes (cycling and speed-skating)
   B. Hayley Wickenheiser (hockey and cycling)
   C. Sue Holloway (Nordic skiing and cycling)

Great Girls Quiz Answers

Scoring: Two points for each right answer.

Soccer

1 (c)

Ten players in the game plus one of the most important people on the field—the goalkeeper.

2 (b)

She, and she alone, can throw the ball back into play. Others can only kick, dribble, and head.

3 (a)

One of the offence's jobs is to try to get the ball within striking distance of the opposition's goal, while the defence stays back to guard their own strike zone.

4 (c)

Depending on the kind of kick, it could be both. Usually, the side of the foot is used in passing the ball, while the top of the foot (laces) is used for a shot.

5 (a)

As in a golf shot, you get underneath the ball and "chip" it over to the player you wish to pass to, in the process getting it over the opposition.

6 (c)

Just watch the soccer greats do this combination, and then practise it yourself.

1–4 points: You can do it. Just keep dribbling a few more times into the rule book, or ask your coach next time you see her.

5–8 points: You know your stuff. A few more headers and you're there.
9–12 points: Soccer Queen!

CANOEING

1 (a)
This is where the Red River and the Assiniboine River meet. People paddled here from the Atlantic, the Pacific, and the Arctic oceans for trade.

2 (b)
Portage and Main is known as the coldest corner in Canada. Once, paddlers had to portage their canoes from either the Red or the Assiniboine rivers to get to the main trading fort, which was about a kilometre away from "the Forks," where the two rivers meet. From the fort, paddlers could carry their canoes or supplies via a portage trail if they wanted to get to the other river without having to go back to the Forks.

When Winnipeg started building roads at the turn of the twentieth century, they named one of their longest streets after this portage trail.

3 (c)

4 (a)
Cedar dugouts are the traditional canoes of the First Nation people of the West Coast. A cedar would be felled and left for several years until it became buoyant and light in water. The person making the canoe would take great care when digging out the cedar, and would thank the tree for allowing the paddlers to use it for transportation and war.

5 (a)
Recreational canoeists aren't in a big rush, and like to appreciate their beautiful surroundings. They may also

paddle through rough waters and rapids. It doesn't make sense for them to use a sleek and aerodynamic boat, which can be so tippy and fragile that even a rock can puncture it. Masts and sails belong to sailboats, but a canoe with a bottom that is somewhat flat and stable will take a recreational canoeist through the most wonderful bodies of water.

6 (a)

Don't ever overcrowd a boat. This is a good way to risk capsizing and drowning. Usually there are two paddlers in a recreational canoe, but sometimes one or two people can sit in the middle and help paddle.

1–4 points: Keep paddling. You'll hit the rapids once you practise those strokes some more.
5–8 points: Just a few more strokes and then let the current carry you.
9–12 points: You must have *coureur de bois* blood in you.

Track and Field

1 (b)

Women were not allowed to run the marathon until 1984. The International Olympic Committee and the International Amateur Athletic Association (which had virtually all-male memberships) declared that women were too frail and weak to run twenty-six miles. In the early 1970s, women starting running marathons to prove both organizations wrong, but it still took over ten years to convince these organizations that women could do it.

2 (c)

3 (c)

The 800 metres begins with a bit of a staggered start. Runners in the outside lanes are a little farther forward than those in the inside lanes. As soon as the gun sounds, runners start to move closer to the inside lanes, and by the first curve, all runners are in the two inside lanes. All races longer than 800 metres start this way. The 400 metres, 200 metres, 100 metres, and hurdles, have staggered starts because runners are not allowed to change into the inside lanes.

4 (b)

In 1928, Canada sent Myrtle Cook, Bobbie Rosenfeld, Florence Bell, and Ethel Smith to the Amsterdam Olympics. Women athletes were only allowed to contest a few sporting events, and relay was one of them. With Myrtle Cook as the anchor runner, the team flew around the track and set a world record in 48.4 yards (distances were measured in yards then). These women started a tradition: Canadian 4x100 relay teams won medals for the next three Olympics.

5 (c)

Debbie started jumping at age nine. By the time she was fourteen, she had invented a new way of clearing the bar: she would run up to the bar facing it, but after jumping, she would turn her body in the air and go over the bar head first—her back clearing it before her legs. Before this, people had jumped the bar with a scissor kick, or had gone sideways over it so their body was parallel to it. This new method of clearing the bar was called "the Brill Bend." Around the same time, an American named Dick Fosbury came up with the same technique, which was dubbed "the Fosbury Flop." Both high jumpers are responsible for inventing the jump that has revolutionized the event.

Debbie Brill went on to set a world record of 1.99 metres in 1982.

6 (b)
Ethel Catherwood was a beautiful young woman from Saskatchewan who represented Canada at the 1928 Olympics in Amsterdam. But the most impressive thing about her was her ability to jump. She won the gold medal in high jump with a leap of 1.59 metres. She had earlier set a world record with a 1.6-metre jump.

1–4 points: Keep jogging that track, you're approaching the curve.
5–8 points: Hey, you cleared the bar.
9–12 points: You've got a fast start off those blocks!

Hockey

1 (b)
Adding an extra player can actually increase the possibility of scoring on the other team. Keeping your goalie in the game can't help the team win, as a good goalie can only try to not allow any more goals from occurring.

2 (c)
Toronto's Geraldine Heaney has played on the national women's team since the first women's international tournament in Ottawa in 1987. She was named to the Canadian team for the first official Women's World Championships in 1990, and retired only after she won an Olympic gold medal at the Salt Lake City Games in 2002.

3 (a)

4 (b)
In 1956 when Abby Hoffman was nine, she was the star of the local hockey team. Her father had signed her up as Ab Hoffman and no one questioned whether she was a boy or a girl. But at the championships that year, her parents had to

provide her birth certificate. When officials found out that Abby was a girl, they barred her from boys' hockey. Abby went on to become a Canadian champion in track and field, and broke the Olympic record for the 800 metres at the Munich Olympics in 1972. She finished eighth, but was less than 1.5 seconds behind the gold medallist.

Abby continued to try to make things better for girls and women in sport and eventually became the Director General for Sport Canada—a position that made her responsible for much of sport in Canada. To pay tribute to her, the Canadian Hockey Association named the national championship trophy after her.

5 (c)
Shannon Miller was a Calgary police officer and an international-level hockey coach when the Canadian Hockey Association hired her to coach the Olympic team in 1997. Shannon took the team to a silver medal at the 1998 Winter Games in Nagano. In 1999, she accepted the position of head coach at the University of Minnesota in Duluth. Since 2001, her team has won every NCAA Championship in women's hockey.

6 (b)
Manon Rheaume had played against boys all her life back in Lac Beauport, Quebec, and wanted to see how far she could take her talent. She played for the farm team of the Tampa Bay Lightning—the Knoxville Cherokee—in 1994. Manon debuted against NHL players in an exhibition game for the Lightning against the St. Louis Blues in September 1992. In that game, she let in two goals in the first period, but so did the Blues' goalie. St. Louis eventually won 6–4. Later she also played for the Nashville Knights, and from 1994 to 1997, for the Canadian national team.

1–4 points: Keep stickhandling, you're going to score soon.
5–8 points: Nice assist.
9–12 points: Great hat-trick!

Basketball

1 (c)

At the end of 1999, Canadian sports writers decided that the men's national hockey team that played in the 1972 Canada Cup series would be Canada's team of the century. They were wrong. The '72 team doesn't hold a candle to the legendary Edmonton Grads. The Grads played their first game in 1915 and their last in 1940—a total of 622 games of which they won 502. They won the first Canadian championships in 1922, and continued to win for another eighteen years. The Grads played America and other international teams in exhibition sports at the Olympics, winning gold in 1924, 1928, 1932, and 1936. They couldn't win an official gold medal since basketball did not become an official Olympic sport for women until 1976.

The Edmonton Grads had to disband in 1940, when their gym was turned into an Air Force base during the Second World War.

2 (b)

Sylvia was a star player as a girl, and she graduated to the national team in 1974, two years before the Montreal Olympics. For ten years, she was voted one of Canada's strongest players, and in 1979, she was the MVP at the World Championships. That year, the Canadian team won bronze at the Pan-Am Games and the Student World Games in Mexico. Sylvia retired after the 1984 Olympics to pursue a career in film and television.

3 (a)
One point. However, you can do two foul shots if you are fouled in the act of shooting, worth one point each. The only time you get one shot is when you are fouled, the shot goes in, and then the ref awards you with one full-throw foul shot. So, technically, you could get three points on one foul.

4 (c)
You can't move on the floor with the ball unless you are dribbling the ball.

5 (c)
In 1948, the Western Canadian Champions in women's basketball boarded a train in Cardston, Alberta, and came to Toronto to play against the Montgomery Maids. The Cardston team had some excellent players, but in the end, the Montgomery Maids won out and brought back the Underwood Trophy, after it had spent many years with the Edmonton Grads in the west.

6 (b)
"Your check" is technically the most correct answer. Sometimes people like to substitute other words, but this can be confusing in the middle of a game.

1–4 points: You're going to sink a free-throw soon, if you practise.
5–8 points: You've almost tied the game.
9–12 points: What a great 3-pointer shot you have!

Cycling

1 (c)
Think about "cranking" the pedals around when referring to this part of the bike. Screw in the crank arms. (Make sure you have the left pedal on the left crank arm and the right

pedal on the right crank arm.) There is no such thing as a pedal arm on a bike, while the drive train consists of the front and rear derailleurs, the chain, the chain rings at the front derailleur, and the freewheel at the back derailleur.

2 (b)

Women cyclists were finally allowed into the Olympics in 1984, but even then only on the road. In 1988, one track event was open to them. At each Olympics, the IOC added one more event, but things are still not equal. There is no team pursuit or Keiren events for women on the track, and a maximum of only three women are allowed from each country in the road race as against a maximum of five men. Women must also ride shorter distances.

3 (c)

Though road racers Clara Hughes and Sue Palmer like to ride their mountain bikes for fun, Alison Sydor rides both international road races and mountain bike races. She has won more World Championships and World Cups than any other mountain biker. She also won a bronze medal at the World Road Championships in 1991.

4 (a)

When your elbows are slightly bent, you can relax your arms and shoulders and have a comfortable ride. Your bike is too big if you have to straighten your arms to reach the handlebars, and too small if your elbows are bent at a 45-degree angle or more. Bikes that are too big are hard to control and inefficient, while those that are too small are uncomfortable.

5 (b)

Always have your weight well back on a downhill in mountain biking unless you enjoy going over the bars! Be careful on the brakes: don't ever slam the brakes on a downhill, but apply more pressure to the back than to the front.

6 (a)
Clara Hughes won two bronze medals at the 1996 Summer Olympics—one in the road race and the other in the time trial. At the 2002 Salt Lake City Olympics, she won a bronze in the 5,000-metre speed-skating event. Clara is the only Canadian, and one of only four athletes in Olympic history, to have achieved this.

1–4 points: Don't worry, on the way home you will have the wind at your back.
5–8 points: It doesn't matter—uphills or downhills, you like them both.
9–12 points: Hey, you're leading the pack!

Where to Find Your Sport

Aboriginal Sport Circle
www.aboriginalsportcircle.ca
Roundpoint Memorial Building
R.R. #3
Akwesasne Mohawk Territory
Cornwall Island, Ontario
K6H 5R7
Tel: 613-938-1176 Fax: 613-938-9181
Executive Director Rick Brant, ext. 22
E-mail: rbrant@aboriginalsportcircle.ca

Athletics Canada
www.athleticscanada.com
2197 Riverside Drive, Suite 300
Ottawa, Ontario
K1H 7X3
Tel: 613-260-5580 Fax: 613-260-0341
E-mail: athcan@athletics.ca

Canadian Association for the Advancement of Women and Sport and Physical Activity
www.caaws.ca
N202 - 801 King Edward Avenue
Ottawa, Ontario
K1N 6N5
Tel: 613-562-5667 Fax: 613-562-5668
E-mail: caaws@caaws.ca

Where to Find Your Sport

Canadian Cycling Association
www.canadian-cycling.com
702-2197 Riverside Drive
Ottawa, Ontario
K1H 7X3
Tel: 613-248-1353 Fax: 613-248-9311
E-mail: general@canadian-cycling.com

Canadian Recreational Canoeing Association
www.paddlingcanada.com
PO Box 398, 446 Main Street West
Merrickville, Ontario
K0G 1N0
Tel: 613-269-2910 Toll Free: 1-888-252-6292
Fax: 613-269-2908
E-mail: info@paddlingcanada.com

Canadian Soccer Association
www.canadasoccer.com
Place Soccer Canada
237 Metcalfe Street
Ottawa, Ontario
K2P 1R2
Tel: 613-237-7678 Fax: 613-237-1516
E-mail: mini@soccercan.ca

Canadian Tae Kwon Do Association
1300 Carling Avenue
Ottawa, Ontario
K1Z 7L2
Tel: 613-722-6133

Canadian Wheelchair Basketball Association
www.cwba.ca
2211 Riverside Drive, Suite B2
Ottawa, Ontario
K1H 7X5
Tel: 613-260-1296 Fax: 613-260-1456
E-mail: cwba@cwba.ca

Cross Country Canada
http://canada.x-c.com
CCC National Office
Bill Warren Training Centre
1995 Olympic Way, Suite 100
Canmore, Alberta
T1W 2T6
Tel: 403-678-6791 Fax: 403-678-3644
E-mail: info@cccski.com

Hockey Canada
www.hockeycanada.ca
Calgary Office
Father David Bauer Arena
2424 University Drive NW
Calgary, Alberta
T2N 3Y9
Tel: 403-777-3636 Fax: 403-777-3635

Ottawa Office
801 King Edward Avenue, Suite N204
Ottawa, Ontario
K1N 6N5
Tel: 613-562-5677 Fax: 613-562-5676

Where to Find Your Sport

Paralympics Ontario
www.paralympicsontario.ca
1185 Eglinton Avenue East, Suite 102
Toronto, Ontario
M3C 3C6
Tel: 416-426-7187 Toll Free: 1-800-265-1539
Fax: 416-426-7361
E-mail: info@paralympicsontario.ca

Speed Skating Canada
www.speedskating.ca
2781 Lancaster Road, Suite 402
Ottawa, Ontario
K1B 1A7
Tel: 613-260-3669 Fax: 613-260-3660
E-mail: ssc@speedskating.ca

Women's Sports Foundation
www.womenssportsfoundation.org
Eisenhower Park
East Meadow, NY 11554
Toll Free: 1-800-227-3988 (U.S. Only)
Tel: 516-542-4700 (Business)
Fax: 516-542-4716
E-mail: wosport@aol.com